1100 MILES
MONTY

To Brenda

1100 MILES WITH MONTY

SECURITY AND INTELLIGENCE AT TAC HQ

NORMAN KIRBY

SUTTON PUBLISHING

This book was first published in 1989 by
Sutton Publishing Limited · Phoenix Mill
Thrupp · Stroud · Gloucestershire · GL5 2BU

This edition first published in 2003

British Library Cataloguing in Publication Data
A catalogue record for this book is available from the British
Library.

ISBN 0 7509 3428 X

Typeset in 11/12.5pt Photina.
Typesetting and origination by
Sutton Publishing Limited.
Printed and bound in Great Britain by
J.H. Haynes & Co. Ltd, Sparkford.

CONTENTS

ACKNOWLEDGEMENTS

For permission to publish extracts from the *Memoirs* of Field Marshal Montgomery grateful acknowledgement is made to A.P. Watt Limited on behalf of Viscount Montgomery of Alamein, CBE.

I also wish to thank Captain J. Barry of the Ministry of Defence for allowing publication of the book in its present form.

I am greatly indebted to friends and relations who, with their interest in the subject, encouraged me to persevere in the work. Among these are individuals and families in France, Belgium and Holland, who not only supplied me with information about conditions in their countries during the years of occupation, but entertained me with generous hospitality. Mention must be made of François and Marie Louis Hamel, Inge and Hilmar van den Bosch, Klaas Schol, and Moris and Albine (née Gennotte) Gergeay, from whom I have received not only great kindness but invaluable practical help. Ironically the turbulent years of our first meetings are among my most cherished memories.

I am grateful too for wartime comrades and for the unique job which made all these friendships possible.

Nita McCrossen spent hours in photocopying the typescript. For this and for constant encouragement I express my sincere appreciation and gratitude.

For the physical emergence of the manuscript from my amateur typing to its present appearance I offer my thanks to the staff of Sutton Publishing, especially to Sarah Flight for her careful advice and the all those who contributed to its publication.

PREFACE

In the course of the work described in this book one unremarkable life came, all too briefly, into collision with heroic men and women caught up in the tensions and exertions of wartime resistance. Life in the armed forces, backed by the support of a resolute nation, the framework of command, and the daily comfort of cheerful comrades, cannot be compared in any way with the lonely, nerve-racking struggle of civilians in an occupied country against an alien and cruel enemy.

Though my knowledge of them during the years of occupation and in my own brief encounters is only partial, I honour the memory of Fernand Gennotte, Inge van den Bosch, Elizabeth Schol, Maria de Meyer and two brave English nuns, Mère Majella and Mère Ursule of the Ursuline Convent in Hasselt. I can never forget them. These are people who, among many others, have given life, limbs, health and sanity so that out cherished way of life might survive. This is my excuse for writing about my own experiences in a time of war.

PREFACE TO THE FIRST PAPERBACK EDITION

THE SIXTIETH ANNIVERSARY OF D-DAY 2004

The days before departure for Normandy were fraught with uncertainty. I was to meet Denise Williams, whom I had met only once before, on the boat. We were both to receive the veterans' medals (she in honour of her husband) from the mayor of the small country town of Thaon, north-west of Caen. At Ouistreham, the port for Caen, we were to separate, and I was to be met by Monsieur and Madame Le Marchand, my host and hostess, whom I had never met before.

Strangely, many features of this journey recalled the historic one of 1944. On both occasions I had to be on board on 4 June. On both occasions the weather was atrocious, the sky threatening, and the sea mountainous. There were differences. There was no need to wear tin hat, heavy boots, gas mask or loaded pack. No machine guns or bayonets awaited us on the other side. But in 1944, without being a hero, and having so much to do, I don't remember feeling afraid, only intoxicated with excitement – and very sick! Instead of one lonely French widow, I had tens of thousands of comrades for company, and that pillar of confidence, General Montgomery with his Christian God of battles as our guides. And I was young!

I need not have worried. At the moment of entering the boat, Denise and I almost collided with each other. And there at Ouistreham promptly at 10.30 p.m. were Raymond and Julienne Le Marchand waiting to greet me, with outstretched arms and smiles of welcome. Denise and I parted company, and I was whisked off into the dark, sweet-smelling countryside to a beautiful house in Tourville-sur-Odon, in the heart of rural Normandy, south-west of Caen. A wonderful meal awaited me, restoring strength and wellbeing.

On Sunday 5 June, after a service in church and a ceremony at the war memorial, four of us – Denise and I and two Canadian veterans – received our medals. There was no mistaking the warmth of the received our medals. There was no mistaking the warmth of the welcome at Thaon, from the speeches of Pierre Paunet the mayor (in French) and of the deputy mayor (in English) to the certificates and diplomas making us 'citoyens de la commune de Thaon' and many unexpected gifts. The celebrations were rounded off by the traditional 'vin d'honneur' followed by a festive dinner with the mayor's family. That unforgettable 5 June marked the close of my own formal ceremony.

Then came the fiftieth anniversary of D-Day itself. The climax came in the afternoon of 6 June when we gathered on the wet sand at Arromanches for the visit of H.M. the Queen and the Royal Family and the march past of veterans. On a day when the armed forces were in the limelight it was fitting that the Queen, in honouring the veterans, paid tribute to the French Resistance, represented on the royal dais in the person of Simone Veil, a former concentration camp victim. The march past of hundreds of veterans, male and female, and widows, some of them marching stoutly through water, was one of the most moving demonstrations of patriotic pride that I have ever seen. Hundreds more veterans were among the thousands of spectators who thronged the beach and covered the cliffs and hills of Arromanches like a vast swarm of bees. At the sight of the marchers a Frenchman next to me said, 'C'est grandiose'. Emotions ranged from joy to sorrow, from elation to wistfulness as people, French and British alike, joined in the singing and rhythmical hand-clapping in time with the marching feet and the military bands, skilfully synchronised with each other, as each in turn entered, with renewed applause into prominence.

As we left the beach to walk back through the town, the French population hemmed in on both sides of the street by barriers lining the kerbs, thrust their arms forward to shake our hands and say, 'Thank you for saving our country', 'Thank you for saving France', 'Thank you for the liberation'. With so many expressions of gratitude, I could not help wondering what thoughts were occupying the minds of the people of Aunay-sur-Odon which was totally erased fifty years ago.

For the rest of my stay I was taken on a tour of the countryside as each commune vibrated to the sound of church bells and military music. Flags of the Allies were everywhere, decorating even the tiniest hamlets and the remotest cottages. Children crowded round us to collect autographs, in school exercise books, on little scraps of paper, one boy asking me to write my name on his T-shirt. Then came visits to some scenes of the fiercest battles of the war, now completely rebuilt and unrecognisable: Villers-Bocage, Tilly-sur-Seulles, Le Mollay-Littry, Balleroy where a shellburst had shattered my left ear, and finally Blay where, on François Hamel's farm, Monty had his longest stay before the fall of Caen on 9 July 1944. It was here I was told about the Montgomery Monument to be unveiled on 23 June (the fiftieth anniversary of the date when we moved our camp from Creully to Blay). I was urged to return for this ceremony, though going home on the morrow.

NORMANDY REVISITED

After my arrival home from Normandy on 10 June, there followed an interval of ten days during which I had respite to rest and think about the possibility of returning for the unveiling of the Montgomery Monument. I decided to go, not realising what this decision would entail.

Approaching the coast of Normandy while it was still daylight (at 10.30 p.m. French time), I tried to recapture, in my mind, that first landing in 1944. The effort of recalling the immensity of the seascape, and the vast expanse of the beaches, invaded by thousands of servicemen, accompanied by the ear-splitting din of battle, was difficult indeed on that peaceful summer evening as we glided silently into Ouistreham. Once again my friends were awaiting me, and again on arrival was the welcome meal.

The proceedings at Blay started with lunch in the beautiful, centuries-old stone farmhouse of the President of the Montgomery Monument Association, Monsieur de Bourdon de Gramont. At this luncheon I met Trevor Martin, Monty's personal pilot, and his wife. We had last seen each other at Blay in 1944 when I had needed to persuade the farmer, François Hamel, to set aside a field for the airstrip.

In the afternoon there were interviews for French television, then various notable personalities started to arrive: Monsieur le Député, Monsieur le Sous-Préfet, the Mayor of Blay, Madame

Cambron, Monsieur Bénamou, historian and curator of the Bayeux Museum, representatives of the French Army, the American Embassy, the Director of Tourism, the press and the police. Twenty standard bearers (French veterans), a band and many people from surrounding villages gathered at the steps of the first monument. This was at a road junction and marked the site associated with the name of Montgomery, his camp at Blay being the midpoint between the US and British armies, of which he was commander. The second monument was in the form of a black marble orientation table, indicating the position of Tac HQ, the place where we lived for six weeks before Caen was finally and painfully liberated. At the first monument there were speeches from the Mayor of Blay, the Député, the Sous-Préfet, and the laying of wreaths, one by Trevor and me, and bunches of flowers from the children.

Then came an extraordinary introduction: Monsieur Bénamou, curator of the Bayeux Museum, approached me and said, 'I want you to meet again someone whom you first met fifty years ago in a bicycle shop in Bayeux'. It was Guillaume Mercader, leader of Resistance, to whom I had been secretly introduced in the backroom of his bicycle shop in 1944. He remembered me as the first British soldier he had met after the Normandy landings.

At the second monument Trevor and I were called upon to do the unveiling, and I made a speech. The quiet country lanes of Blay resounded to the music of the trumpets blaring forth God Save the Queen, the Stars and Stripes and La Marseillaise. The whole assembly then made its way downhill towards the church accompanied by newspaper reporters, to the vin d'honneur, this time in the open air, with food and wine decorously laid out on trestle tables in the school playground. The sun shone that day as it had rarely done in the weeks before.

Early the next morning, after emotional good-byes, Trevor, Marit his wife, and I sat on the deck of the *Duc de Normandie* watching the Normandy coast gradually disappear amid memories that are hardly ever likely to share the same fate.

Belgium Fifty Years Later, 1994

The invitation had come from Nandy's sister, Albine, and brother-in-law, Moris to attend the fiftieth anniversary celebrations of Belgium's liberation.

Saturday 3 September for the commemoration of Belgian Resistance, was a beautiful, sunny day, as it needed to be for so much outdoor movement. Starting at 2.30 p.m. from the Grand Place in Péruwelz, the population of this active centre of wartime resistance paid homage to those who had perished at the hands of the Gestapo. A roll on the drums was the signal for quiet to begin the various acts of remembrance at all the different places in town and country, marked now by permanent monuments where the victims had lost their lives. Some of them had died on the day of the liberation itself, and others in May 1945, in Germany, with the war almost over. From the first monument in the town square we proceeded on our pilgrimage, in a lengthy procession of private cars and coaches, with police escorts and standard bearers to the many other monuments which pin-pointed the scenes of violent death. There were monuments of varied design, according to the wishes of family and friends, at street corners, in the middle of a field, at a farm, alongside the canal, adjoining what is now the motorway, (Nandy's monument). At each monument the ceremony was the same: drums, laying of flowers by family and friends, history of events, a moment of silence, sound of the trumpet, the Last Post, drums. Then the move to the next destination, with much getting in and out of cars, much standing in postures of respectful silence, and not a few tears.

The last monument to be visited was that of Nandy Gennotte. This was a large, impressive block of granite bearing an inscription in brass. Resting against it was a photograph of Nandy. It was covered with the Belgian flag, for this was to be a ceremony of inauguration as well as commemoration. The unveiling was performed by the hero's sister, Albine, and the senator burgomaster. This was followed by the laying of flowers, some of them by three officers of the RAF whom we would meet again on Sunday.

Just one or two fo the histories recounted at the memorials typify many of those events of 1944, though each has its own individual poignancy and horror. On the day of liberation three young men, hearing a vehicle entering the square mistakenly ran out to greet the 'Allies'. It belonged to retreating Germans who opened fire. What remains is a plaque on the wall against which the flowers are heaped. Another youth, aged 18, pursued across a field by the Gestapo who aimed their fire at his legs, realised he could not escape, and rather than be captured alive, shot himself.

Sunday 4 September was devoted to celebration of the fiftieth anniversary of Belgium's liberation. It started with Solemn Mass in commemoration of heroes who had died for their country, in the magnificent church of Saint Quentin in Péruwelz. Because we were 'attached' to a Resistance family we were ushered to the front pews close by the altar. Enlarged photographs of the dead resistants were fixed to each of the pillars of the church. The choir, high up in the gallery of the organ loft, gave us a feast of music from Handel, Mozart, Gounod, Saint-Saëns, Gregorian chant, and some modern compositions. During Communion I recognised by compatriots from the RAF.

After the service, struggling not to get lost in the crowd, we walked, again in procession, to the War Memorial, decorated with the flags of all the Allies. A short ceremony with an address by the mayor, flowers, trumpets, drums and a benediction by the priest ended with the appropriate national anthems.

At a given signal the cortège formed up again in its strict order and made its way to the Park and Monument of the Resistance. This is a remarkable model in stone of two hands caught in the act of casting off the chains that bind them. Beneath them are the words:

Nous, les soldats de l'ombre
Nous avons résisté
Pour que de la pénombre
Jaillisse la clarté

We, the soldiers of the darkness
We have resisted
So that out of the shadows
May burst the light

Then came the familiar sequence of events: the drums, the flowers, given by different associations, including a wreath by Flight Sergeant William Murdoch of No 59 Squadron, RAF, shot down at Maubray on 18 May 1940; a historical narrative by the President of the Amicale des Associations Patriotiques of the activities of the resistants killed by the enemy; and a recitation in English by Squadron Leader Donald McLeod of No 56 Squadron, RAF, shot down at Wadelincourt on 16 May 1940, from Laurence Binyon's poem, *For the Fallen*: 'They shall grow not old, as we that are left grow old . . .' He broke down and could not continue.

The same poem, with its exhortation, 'We will remember them,' was then recited in French by Donald's Belgian friend, Monsieur Nachez. The Last Post, sounded after this was almost too emotional for some of those present. The choir of Saint Quentin's church rounded off the proceedings with the Chant des Partisans. Then the drums. The vin d'honneur and the signing of the Livre d'Or (the Golden Book), to be deposited later in the Town Hall, marked the end of the official business.

After another look at Nandy's monument the Gennotte family journeyed on for lunch to Bon Secours, a town on Belgium's frontier with France. At the end of the meal, while we were drinking coffee, an elderly lady from the next table came up to me (obviously the only Englishman there) and said, 'Do you mind if I kiss you, Monsieur?'

'Non Madame!'

She then said, to my embarrassment, 'It's because of you that we are here in freedom.'

'And because of a few million others,' I thought.

She continued, 'In 1940 an RAF plane crashed over our town which was surrounded by German troops, and the young pilot landed by parachute in our back garden. He was distressed and bewildered, not knowing where he was. I went to him and said, "Don't worry, you are among friends. I will take you to a safe house."

'There were many German soldiers in the town. My husband came in the garden at that moment, and said to me, "No. You stay here. I will take the young man."'

She never saw or heard of her husband again.

1
PROLOGUE

Today it is difficult to imagine life as it was in 1940 when in Britain food and clothing were rationed and even the simplest commodities and services, now taken for granted, did not exist. It was a world without supermarkets, launderettes, plastic bags, biros, sellotape, long-playing records, transistors or tape-recorders and neither the Beatles nor television had yet made their revolutionary impact on the entertainment scene. Few families possessed a car and bananas were on the list of unobtainable, exotic fruits. There were no packaged holidays by air and the huge civilian airports at Heathrow and Gatwick did not exist. The welfare state would not be formed until 1948 and there were no statutory primary or junior schools. Other world events had not yet changed the consciousness of mankind forever; no news had leaked out about the full horror of the Nazi holocaust, and no atomic bomb had yet destroyed people's confidence in the future of the planet. Young people were still able to give vent to patriotic feelings singing: 'There'll be bluebirds over the white cliffs of Dover', and 'There'll always be an England' with a mixture of optimism and wistfulness.

In the summer of 1942, 400 million people in Europe were under Nazi domination. From the Channel ports of France to the shores of the Black Sea and from the Mediterranean to the Arctic, Hitler was in control; Switzerland had maintained her neutrality and only Britain and Russia remained to be added to the Third Reich. It was therefore a time of feverish preparation for the population of both these countries, and when Russia was the first to

1

attack Stalin, in the determined effort to force the Germans to fight on two fronts, appealed to the British Government for a second front to be opened in the west. It was now, two years after Dunkirk, that 'Open the Second Front Now' began to appear scrawled on walls and bridges by Communist and Russian sympathizers. Britain was therefore committed to two kinds of preparation: defensive, against the German invasion of these islands, and offensive for our invasion of Europe. All hopes were pinned upon the 'Second Front' – D-Day. It was a time of record output on the labour front, of neighbourliness and comradeship, of scarcity and sacrifice.

The war effort was accepted by the majority of the population in this country as a necessary evil. Though not wildly demonstrative, there were occasions when, stirred by the voice of Winston Churchill, they felt themselves to be engaged in a crusade against the powers of darkness; but the prevailing mood was one of 'getting on with it', a dogged spirit which eventually brought victory. But whatever the level of patriotic fervour, a win for Hitler was unthinkable, and the Nazi war machine threatening to engulf the whole world had to be stopped.

The preparation and training of individual citizens for the possible invasion of their homeland took a variety of forms, now seemingly incredible. Staid ratepayers in humdrum jobs along with their more bohemian and colourful contemporaries found themselves pitch-forked into uniforms and Nissen huts, doing PT before breakfast, foot-slogging on route marches, swinging ape-like from trees on a battle course or immersed up to the waist in cold water fixing barbed wire entanglements in the sea. This last predicament was one in which I found myself many times, as a Sapper in the Royal Engineers, together with arms drill, digging trenches, making roads, coal-heaving and dabbling with demolitions and high explosives. After two years, thanks to having been a schoolmaster at Dartford Grammar School where I taught French and German, I found myself, in

1942, in the Intelligence Corps following a course in counter-sabotage which also involved training as a saboteur. We learned how to detect and set booby-traps, how to recognise and detonate mines, how to force an entry into a protected building and to penetrate the most formidable fortifications. For the next eight months six of us were cast in the role of German saboteurs. Our task was to test the security of public utilities – power stations, gasworks and reservoirs – by forcing an entrance and 'blowing them up or otherwise putting them out of action.' Total destruction of a power station was achieved by placing our plasticine 'bombs', which looked very like gelignite, inside the most sensitive part of the generator. Every raid was followed by a detailed report and recommendations for the improvement of security. Freddie Hensby and I worked together and covered all the power stations in the London area, Birmingham and the Midlands, Scotland and Wales. We managed to complete this task, but D-Day intervened before we could embark on the gasworks and reservoirs, and other duties beckoned. The security of each power station had to be tested in two different ways: first by trying to go in by the main gate in daylight, using forged documents and false identity cards, and second by testing the perimeter and its physical defences at night. For the daytime raids we were kitted out with dark suits, Anthony Eden hats and briefcases, using alibis of our own invention such as officers of the Ministry of Home Security, Fire Prevention Service, Home or War Office. At night we became burglars, breaking in over unclimbable railings, electrified fences and barbed wire, occupations for which our course of training on detachment with MI5 and Scotland Yard stood us in good stead. We wore boiler suits or dungarees, blacked our faces, and if caught were either dumb or growled something in German.

It was eight months of nightmare. As we were on detachment from our army unit we had to find our own accommodation. For our nocturnal escapades we could choose only the most disreputable lodgings in the poorest parts of town, whether in London, Birmingham, Glasgow, Edinburgh or Cardiff. Sometimes the beds were so filthy that we slept on top of them, fully dressed, and just removed our boots. Even today, forty years later, I still have a clear-cut memory of those anxious nights; being chased by alsations at Yoker in Clydebank, getting caught up on the electrified fence at Battersea, facing the bayonets of the Home Guard in Dundee and jumping into the icy river in Cardiff with armed troops in hot pursuit. One escape caused me to fall backwards into an eight foot deep concrete hole at the newly extended power station at Cambuslang and landed me in Glasgow Infirmary. Hensby suffered a bayonet wound during the same series of night raids in Scotland, and it was while we were incarcerated in Dundee gaol that, because of this injury and the need for medical treatment, we decided to give ourselves up.

We did, however, have almost total success in Scotland where we managed to plant all our bombs and achieve complete 'destruction' of all the Scottish power stations except for Dundee. Here the alert and watchful workers came after us with sledge-hammers, crowbars, and any weapons they could lay their hands on. Woe betide a German saboteur in Dundee!

We worked in pairs. One of us placed the bomb, the other kept watch. We took it in turns. Of the two jobs, keeping watch was the more disagreeable: tension without action, responsibility without control. On that night in Dundee I kept watch. The inside of the power station was lit by one electric light bulb. As Freddie entered the generating room I saw, with dismay, a creeping black shadow the size of an elephant projected on to the whitewashed wall. Immediately the loud noise of a bell from inside the building followed by the Home Guard alarm outside broke the silence of the night and a startled Hensby shot past me with lightning speed, hissing:

'They've seen me.'

The Home Guard were already forming up and without delay bore down upon the scene of the 'crime'. A pile of bricks stood against the power station wall. I crouched down behind it. The marching feet came nearer, then passed my hiding-place. With a feeling of relief I stood up, only to see one rearguard soldier systematically peering behind every obstacle with the aid of a torch. I crouched down again as low as possible. Suddenly a pool of light flooded my hide-out and I felt the warmth of a torch on my neck. In his excitement the voice of the soldier broke into falsetto as he screamed:

'Corporal!'

I heard the command, 'Guard! Halt! About turn! Bayonets fix!' They came on, their weapons at the ready, then I heard the corporal say:

'Be careful, we want the bastard alive not dead.'

Stepping into the open I was seized and my arms pinned behind me, the point of a bayonet in my back. Hensby in his hideaway under a railway truck was in a worse plight as the bayonets probed underneath the wagons from each side of the track. He let out a piercing scream as the steel cut into his side.

It was the police who rescued us by driving us away to gaol in their Black Maria. We were able to keep up our subterfuge until Hensby's obvious pain and discomfort obliged us to hand over the letter from MI5 disclosing our real identity as British soldiers. We learnt later that the alertness of the Dundee workers stemmed from the sighting three weeks earlier of a German U-boat off the coast. We were released from prison and entertained to dinner in the Royal Hotel by the staff of the power station who had been congratulated on their vigilance during the night and were in celebratory mood with champagne and cigars (in war-time). No such warmth greeted us at other power stations where the lack of security invited only warnings and 'rockets' from Whitehall. Some installations, as at Portobello, boasted such impregnable defences that the staff felt able to relax their vigilance inside these boundaries. It was here that inventiveness in breaking in was taxed to the utmost. An intricate mesh of Dannert barbed wire extended for several yards inside the perimeter from the top of the high spiked railings. It was while tramping round the streets of Edinburgh, trying to solve this problem of forced entry into their 'Colditz' that Hensby and I saw a roll of linoleum in an ironmonger's shop. This was the answer: with the linoleum fixed by guy ropes to a telegraph pole near the railings we could slide down it over the barbed wire, and to get out we could use the ropes as reins to walk up the linoleum path to the top of the railings and drop outside on to the pavement again. Our main difficulty was waiting until all traffic and pedestrians had disappeared from this busy thoroughfare and we were alone. It was 2 a.m. when the last courting couple moved away from our telegraph pole and, using our linoleum slipway, we were able to gain a speedy and successful entrance and exit. The only bad moment came when a door suddenly opened, a shaft of light lit up the patch of smooth lawn across which we were creeping, and Hensby was hit in the chest by a packet of sandwiches thrown out and discarded by one of the workers. Although we were caught in the full glare of the light with our 'bombs' at the ready, no one noticed us.

The report of total damage to the installation following this expedition drew attention to the fact that alertness on the part of the staff – as at Dundee with its rotting wooden fence – was more important for security than the strongest and costliest of material defences. A beautifully clipped lawn reaching to the walls of the building may be aesthetically pleasing but from the security point of view gravel would be more likely to betray the approach of possible intruders.

In the south we had less success and a few minor injuries: at Willesden I tore my hands and clothing when I hung suspended for some agonising minutes on the barbed wire before falling and sinking into a mountainous slag heap; and I was sick on the river bank in Cardiff, having plunged into the chill water at 4 a.m. in my efforts to escape from the pursuing guards.

At Battersea we were arrested, and after the raid on Littlebrook Power Station we were handcuffed to policemen and marched in broad daylight down Dartford High Street, much to the surprise of the lunchtime shoppers. I was petrified in case any of the boys or masters should see me when they came out of school. In fact one of the masters, a Mr Woodhouse, did emerge from his favourite café immediately in front of me and the policeman to whom I was handcuffed, but like a restive horse I managed to hang back so as not to overtake him and risk detection, the subsequent stupefaction of the school population and possible scandal. So much for one obscure citizen's part in the defensive aspect of preparation for invasion.

It was soon after this that the other kind of preparation – offensive – affected my life. It has to be admitted that D-Day, when it did come, was not only a breath-taking adventure (I have experienced nothing like it since) but a tremendous relief after the stresses of my previous assignment. I had hated every moment of it, especially the writing of reports which would cause trouble to ordinary people. Not one of the six of us had volunteered for this job as it was simply part of routine security duties, yet I was to appreciate the value of this experience when I found myself on the other side of the picture.

2
D-DAY

In April 1944 I was called for interview at a camp in Southwick Park, near Portsmouth; it was not clear what the job would involve except that all was wrapped in secrecy. There were twelve of us from different army units waiting nervously outside an army hut within this large sealed military establishment. Mine was the first name to be called and, with much misgiving, I rose to my feet and entered the hut. The interview was a noisy and disconcerting one and unlike any other of my experience. An officer stormed in and addressed me aggressively in French, to which I replied as best I could.

'So you've made it!' he bawled.

'Sir?'

'Dammit! Are you deaf?' (Nom de Dieu! Êtes-vous sourd?)

(Ironically I was partially deaf in one ear, and my hearing was to be further impaired by a later excursion in the cause of security.)

'I said,' he shouted, 'You've made it!'

He was at all times indubitably audible.

Not fully understanding whether reference was being made to the punctuality, or otherwise, of my arrival, or to the fact of my having gained an interview at all, there was nothing for it but to agree:

'Yes sir,' I replied, trembling, but trying to keep the voice firm and the body erect.

'What do you think you are doing here?'

He was then interrupted by the noisy eruption into the room of another red-faced officer screaming in German.

8

'Well then! What have we here? (Also! Was haben wir hier?) What gives you the idea that *you* would be any good for this job?' This was said or spat with a mixture of bantering and sarcasm.

Having only just arrived in the place it did not require much intelligence to suppose that I could not have done anything to upset them. Nevertheless, feeling very nervous and shaken by their shower of abuse, I got the impression that they were deliberately aiming to fluster and intimidate me.

'Well,' boomed the French officer, 'you heard what the man said. What qualifies you to come here?'

I still did not know what THE JOB entailed, but hazarded the reply: 'My training sir.'

'Your training? And what is that? (Was ist das?)' roared the German.

'I have to be careful about the people I speak to.'

This was only too true on this occasion, with the added obligation of having to answer in French to the Frenchman and in German to the German.

'Are you being deliberately impertinent?'

The whole conversation on their side was conducted in a series of explosions, and on my side in nervous but reasonably decisive attempts to justify my presence among them.

'What do you mean by that?'

'Explain yourself.'

At this stage they were both shouting at once. Steadied by the thought that I had not actually done anything to provoke such angry outbursts I managed to summon up the courage, or the effrontery, to say:

'And what gives *you* the right to speak to a member of His Majesty's Forces like that?' I asked for proof of their identity.

Defiantly they flung their documents on the table and I discovered, with some relief, that they were faked. The stamp did not cover any part of the man's photograph in either case. I pointed this out and it was then that the most alarming stage of the interview occurred. They abandoned the foreign language test and, in what appeared to be mounting rage, I was rudely dismissed with a loud:

'Get out,' in English.

Feeling my cheeks burning I went through the door in a kind of trance and made my way towards my Matchless motor bike. Just as I was about to kick-start it a voice thundered from the hut:

'Where the hell do you think you're going?'

'Back to my unit, Sir.'

'Who said anything about going? You stay here.'

I sat down again with the other candidates, who looked decidedly sick, having heard the rumpus in the hut. Then the next victim's name was called. When all had been in, I was called back again. My two interviewing officers were all smiles as they informed me that the mysterious job was mine.

I was told later that my two interviewers were in fact distinguished actors. They certainly put on a most convincing performance.

There were more trials to come but I could not then have suspected what they would be. The work was to prove onerous and exacting, but promised unique and exciting opportunities to witness history in the making. I was to be attached to General Montgomery's Tactical Headquarters (known by its intimates as Tac) where I became responsible for security, a task which for an NCO seemed awesome in the extreme.

In that same month a small collection of tents and caravans had begun to form under an avenue of trees in Southwick Park, not far from the huge colony of tents, marquees and huts which was Main Headquarters 21st Army Group. Only a copse separated the two encampments, which in April 1944 were as close to each other as they would ever be; soon the tiny Tactical Headquarters would be starting on its great adventure, the long-expected Second Front, and nothing less than the English Channel would lie between it and Main Headquarters. Once Tac had left the oaks and beeches of Southwick Park it seemed that it was forever wedded to bracken and fir trees, and to the idea of isolation, a strange paradox for a headquarters which, with its buzzing telephone wires, was the most vital nerve-centre of the war, in constant touch with the British Prime Minister and other Allied war leaders.

Perhaps it was its loneliness, its small size, its eccentricity, or the fact that Tac was the wartime home of General Montgomery, that gave to its inhabitants a feeling of belonging to something unique. Tac's contradictory mixture of immunity and accountability was both a reflection of the Commander-in-Chief's independent spirit and a direct implementation of his own method of waging war. As Montgomery said in his *Memoirs*:

> I must mention my system of personal command from a Tactical Headquarters, located well forward in the battle area. I divided my headquarters into three echelons:
>
> | | |
> |---|---|
> | Tac | HQ |
> | Main | HQ |
> | Rear | HQ |
>
> Tac HQ was the headquarters from which I exercised personal command and control of the battle. It was small, highly efficient, and completely mobile on its own transport. It consisted chiefly of signals, cipher, liaison staff, defence troops, and a very small operations staff for keeping in touch with the battle situation.
>
> Main HQ was the central core of the whole headquarters organisation. I gave verbal orders to my subordinate commanders from Tac HQ. . . .
>
> Rear HQ was the administrative echelon of the headquarter organisation.

A soldier whose job in this close-knit team depended upon being watchful could not avoid some observation of Monty's personality as well as of his security. A character which in popular imagination appeared all-of-piece – the uncomplicated man of action – presented some surprises and contradictions. He was a seeker after solitude yet he revelled in the adulation of the public; he was required to be protected by strict security, yet when travelling through busy streets he would tell his driver to slow down in order to be recognised and acknowledge the cheers of the crowd. This habit did not necessarily stem from vanity, as has been suggested, but might have been prompted by consideration for his admirers and the interests of morale. A single-minded commander who often antagonised other high-ranking officers by his opinionatedness, he was at pains to make personal contact among the ranks of his fighting men and to win their trust. An ascetic with an austere life-style, he liked his caravan to be as much like home as possible, with many of the simple comforts of home life, including domestic animals.

The contrasting sides of General Montgomery's character can be seen in his *Memoirs*. He chose solitude in which to work yet made no secret of the fact that he was capable of feeling the pangs of loneliness:

> Some think that morale is best sustained when the British soldier is surrounded by NAAFIs, clubs, canteens, and so on. I disagree. My experience with soldiers is that they are at their best when they are asked to face up to hard conditions. Men dumped in some out-of-the-way spot in the desert will complain less of boredom, because they have to shift for themselves, than those surrounded by a wide choice of amenities.

Tac HQ in its isolation exemplified this way of thinking, and visitors from Main Headquarters grumbled about its being 'out-of-the-way'. According to Monty's reasoning this seclusion gave him the necessary conditions for the careful planning demanded by his conduct of the battle:

> It is absolutely vital that a senior commander should keep himself from becoming immersed in details, and I always

did so. I would spend many hours in quiet thought and reflection in thinking out the major problems.

Yet Monty felt unhappy when excluded:

One thing made me feel lonely. A Thanksgiving Service for the end of the war in Africa was held in St Paul's Cathedral on the 19th May; I was in London but was not asked to attend. It was explained to me *after the service* that it was desired to keep my presence in England a secret. Yet to my delighted surprise, wherever I went I was followed by crowds. The incident made me realise that if I were pretty popular with a lot of people, I was not too popular in some circles. Perhaps the one explained the other.

There was the odd occasion when the strict Puritan image gave way to the popular hero, and Monty, a fanatical non-smoker (insisting on the NO SMOKING rule in any hall where he was due to speak, even to the extent of clearing the building when this rule was infringed), handed out cigarettes to front line troops during his visits to them.

In the final chapter of his *Memoirs*, following references to his team of Liaison Officers, who were the most distinctive vehicle of his method of command, and to his grief over the death of the young John Poston, he returns again to the subject of loneliness:

I suppose that by the time I withdrew from active soldiering I had achieved a certain fame – notoriety, anyway: but I had definitely learnt that the road which leads you there is hard and strewn with rocks, and the route to the summit is difficult. He who reaches the top will often be misunderstood and the target for much criticism; this will produce at times a feeling of loneliness, which is accentuated by the fact that those with whom he would most like to talk will often avoid him because of his position. The only policy in high positions is an intense devotion to duty and the unswerving pursuit of the target, in spite of criticism whispered or in the open. This is what I sought to do.

In the purely military sense General Montgomery was uncompromisingly single-minded. The most conspicuous of all his attributes was his unshakeable confidence in himself, an infectious quality which rapidly spread throughout all ranks of the armed forces and among the general public, British and Allied alike. This strength was linked with a firm, simple faith in God and in the righteousness of the Allied cause. His talks to the troops had a clarity and directness to which they responded with the enthusiasm and practical vigour required for ultimate victory. It was the simplicity and the decisiveness that came across, unclouded by any doubts about the outcome of the war.

As Tac consisted of men from different military units and these were represented by so few individuals, new members were therefore welcomed as sharers in an exceptional enterprise. Even after so many years the memory of that comradeship remains and I still recall with gratitude my companions' concern about the loneliness of my job and the friendly invitation to share their living quarters rather than be in a tent on my own. Although my work involved some uncomfortable secrecy and a strict watchfulness over breaches of security, ('Careless talk costs lives') it never placed any barriers between myself and my 'mates' in the other outfits, nor did it give rise to too much embarrassing inquisitiveness concerning my activities in the field of intelligence. I had soon realised that my most urgent purpose at Tac HQ was to make my rôle acceptable to the men. With some perseverance I was able to break down the 'snooper' image and win their goodwill, cooperation and eventually their friendship. There was some good-humoured teasing, usually at everybody's expense, and a light-hearted tolerance of individual foibles. The men of Tac HQ behaved much as other soldiers did away from home, but they were far from being stereotypes of the fighting man. Not only were their regional origins varied, but their former civilian occupations were equally diverse. Manual and office workers, small businesses, catering, teaching, the arts, music and the theatre were all represented together with a diversity of leisure interests which ranged from boxing to ballet. We shared the same funny stories, the same alarms and excitements, the same spells of boredom, the same sense of waste and irritation with the awfulness of war, and felt ourselves to be part of a team.

Nevertheless General Montgomery, with his immediate staff, lived in a world apart despite being contained within the same small area. His three caravans were usually in a separate field and there was a reverential gap between our camp and the hallowed ground of his enclosure. Even when called to report to the caravan I never completely lost the guilty feeling of being a trespasser. Everything about his living quarters contributed to the idea of seclusion: the tank by the entrance, the armoured car, the immaculate jeep and the caravans themselves, veiled in camouflage netting as if entangled in some giant spider's web.

There were three caravans, two of which had been captured from Italian commanders in North Africa. One caravan, constructed in Italy and mounted on a Lancia chassis, had belonged to General Annabale Bergonzoli (nicknamed 'Electric Whiskers'), who commanded the Italian 23rd Corps and was captured at Beda Fomm, south of Benghazi, in February 1941. It was used by Montgomery's predecessor as commander of the Eighth Army, Lieutenant-General N.M. Ritchie, after the Lancia mounting had been replaced by a British-made Leyland chassis.

When Lieutenant-General Montgomery took command of the Eighth Army in August 1942, this caravan was his home until the end of the North African campaign in May 1943. It was used as his office during the campaigns in Sicily, Italy and north-west Europe after the Eighth Army captured a second Italian-made caravan in Tunisia from

Field Marshal Giovanni Messe, Commander of the First Italian Army, during the final stages of the North African campaign. This later prize became Monty's bedroom for the rest of the war and, in addition to his bed, contained wardrobes, a washbasin and a bath. So attached to it did he become that he asserted: 'I would turn out of this caravan only for two people: the King, George VI, and Winston Churchill.'

This caravan had also been used by Rommel, whose photograph occupied a prominent position on one wall.

The third caravan completes the picture of Montgomery's characteristic method of conducting the war. This was the famous articulated map lorry designed by him and his personal staff as his operational command centre and delivered on him on 17 April 1944 seven weeks before D-Day. It was to this caravan that his Liaison Officers came with their reports of front line developments and on its walls that large maps gave the latest picture of the battle. The map lorry could be blacked out to enable work to continue during the hours of darkness. Also, as Monty's orders to his subordinates were seldom written down, it was equipped with telephones so that he could talk to them directly. He was contemptuous of those who required everything to be in writing:

Operational command in the battle must be direct and personal, by means of visits to subordinate HQ where orders are given verbally. A commander must train his subordinate commanders, and his own staff, to work and act on verbal orders. Those who cannot be trusted to act on clear and concise verbal orders, but want everything in writing, are useless. There is far too much paper in circulation in the Army, and no one can read even half of it intelligently. (*Memoirs*)

What he did like to have in writing, however, were quotations to give him inspiration. Three were pinned up in his caravan. One was the prayer of Sir Francis Drake on the morning of the attack on Cadiz, 1587:

O Lord God, when Thou givest to Thy servants to endeavour any great matter, grant us also to know that it is not the beginning, but the continuing of the same, until it be thoroughly finished, which yieldeth the true glory.

Another was a verse by James Graham, Marquis of Montrose 1612–1650:

He either fears his fate too much,
Or his deserts are small,
Who dare not put it to the touch,
To win or lose it all.

The third quotation was from Shakespeare's *Henry V*, Act IV, Scene I:

O God of battles! steel my soldiers' hearts.

Other conspicuous attractions in our cavalcade included the 'iron lung', a strange coffin-shaped armoured vehicle like a small scout car, intended for use by the Chief in the event of a close encounter with the enemy but disdainfully unused by him. Our progress through north-west Europe was also preceded and followed by motorcycles of all descriptions, among which were the wide-antlered bikes of the American Military Police assigned to us, and my own temperamental Matchless. The quaintness of our convoy was matched by the originality of its crew. I remember, soon after my arrival at Tac, being staggered by the dress of Monty's immediate entourage (could such apparel ever be called a uniform?): the corduroy trousers, sweaters, Paisley scarves, suede boots and non-regulation headgear. I thought of my old RE sergeant-major having his traditional 'heart attack' at the mere thought of 'improper dress'. Overseas, the hardlined view of a soldier's appearance tended to be relaxed and, except for the occasional ceremonial parade as, for example, when we were visited by King George VI or Winston Churchill, the new liberalism began to spread among the rank and file, though not so outrageously as at the top. John Poston, one of General Montgomery's young liaison officers, though always 'correctly' dressed, wore his 11th Hussars beret in a particularly dashing way, with the fullness pulled to the back of his elegant head, as if he were in the turret of a tank or at the helm of a ship, facing to windward.

The prelude to D-Day meant hard work and numerous 'exercises': rehearsals for embarkation, waterproofing of vehicles and checking of equipment, arms and ammunition in readiness for the seaborne invasion of occupied Europe. As I was still on detachment from my Field Security Section, based at St Paul's School, Hammersmith, before my official posting to Tactical Headquarters, my equipment for D-Day was issued from this London unit. A few days before the invasion one of my former colleagues was despatched by motorbike to Southwick Park with two hundred rounds of ammunition for me. They were in a cardboard box strapped to his pillion. During the long, bumpy journey the weight of the bullets eventually wore a hole in the box. On his arrival at Tac HQ we were both dismayed to find that only eleven rounds were left. Thus one hundred and eighty-nine rounds of live ammunition were scattered on the roads between London and Portsmouth. Being reluctant to get him into trouble I failed to report the incident and found myself having to face the armed might of Germany with only eleven rounds of ammunition. I could only hope that some more would be issued in the heat of battle.

During these strenuous days other units of the armed services in Britain were engaged in schemes involving the use of live ammunition and in some cases the evacuation of the civilian population. I remembered similar drastic action being taken two years previously following the scorched earth policy of the Russians at Stalingrad, when while I was still a Sapper in the Royal Engineers I had taken part in preparations to blow up the Isle of Wight, and in another plan to engulf Poole Harbour in a wall of flame, should Hitler decide to invade us.

Many lonely Hampshire lanes, undisturbed for centuries, reverberated in April 1944 to the thunder of tanks and the laboured groan of engines in low gear. Local farm workers would stand, as if bewitched by the long procession of our curious vehicles: lorries of various weights and shapes, tanks, armoured cars, square-shaped all-purpose vehicles called four-by-fours, Humber Snipes, and two incongruous-looking Rolls-Royces, one with its windscreen sloping inwards at the bottom, and the famous caravans: now museum pieces.

Towards the end of May, throughout the days and nights leading up to the invasion, Tac, in common with units concentrated in vast numbers in the south of Britain, made frequent mysterious excursions into the depths of the countryside, pitching its tents and trundling its caravans under the cover of many a beechwood and fir plantation. The resemblance to mystery tours arose from the fact that all signposts and place-names in Britain had been removed, with the object of confusing a possible invader. Men were therefore totally dependent on the map-reading skills of their leaders, who had a difficult assignment, especially at night in the black-out (which included vehicles) when our route lay off the beaten track, across fields or through wooded country. In spite of the confusion due to the absence of landmarks, our schemes were carried out with efficiency and remarkable good humour. There were innumerable convoy rehearsals, embarkation and disembarkation drills, defence projects, alerts, stand-tos and mock attacks by 'enemy' parachutists. All this while my attention was divided between would-be saboteurs, hypothetical agents and collaborators, will-o'-the-wisp paratroops and the very real claims of camp defence. The security of this key headquarters, which included safeguarding barriers against unlawful entry, protection of the physical defences of the perimeter in cooperation with the officer commanding the Defence Company, checking the dependability of all guards, sentries and defence troops, and also ensuring constant vigilance on the part of all members of the headquarters, was my responsibility. In all of these tasks I was backed up by the Military Police. I was required to give lectures on security ('walls have ears'); and other routines such as the inspection of guards and sentries, interviews with the colonel and contact with the police, both military and civil, continued unabated. Lighter moments were provided by 'official' visits to local pubs, canteens and cafés and the quelling of rumours, such as the sudden appearance, usually at night in outlying districts, of nuns in army boots with two days' growth of stubble and thick German accents. This was part of the folklore of the jittery days spent in anticipation of Hitler's imminent invasion of these islands. Added to these duties was the maintenance of a stubborn and rebellious motor bike.

At Southwick Park the serious part of our adventure was relieved by moments of relaxation: housey-housey (now called bingo and claimed to be the only gambling game permitted by the army), drinks in the Mess, some very amateur hockey, long spells of sunbathing and a game of cricket with a team of Wrens (followed by a dinner and dance). With jitterbugging giving a livelier, more athletic flavour to formal dances in the 1940s, it was surprising what agility, sprightliness and even creativeness could be achieved in spite of the thick battledress and heavy boots of the men and the coverall uniforms of the women. The hot feel of rough serge still brings back memories of those army dances.

Some Marines camped close to us had fitted an amplifier to one of the trees in the avenue, and the voices of Bing Crosby and Dinah Shore supplied a musical background to even the lowliest of our activities. The nights were shattered by enemy raids on Portsmouth. We would rise from our tents and from the slit trenches under the trees to watch arcs of gaily-coloured tracers rising in the sky over Portsmouth. Now and again we would hear the sharp ring of shrapnel against the trunk of a tree when the shell bursts came close.

One morning at the beginning of June we rose with the lark, struck tents, packed our kit, loaded the lorries, and the dust of the avenue was churned up for the last time by our wheels as we moved off on our last and greatest 'scheme' – the invasion of Normandy.

At the end of a long and devious journey during which we had nights of broken sleep and strenuous, back-aching days, we moved at last in full marching order into a large sealed camp, set deep in a dark pinewood, and cloistered from the outside world by strong, uncompromising barriers of barbed wire. Here we lived for a few hours in bell tents and were issued with French money (so France was to be the springboard and not, as rumour had it, Portugal, Holland, Denmark or Norway), rations for twenty-four hours, Mae Wests, Tommy Cookers and vomit bags.

That evening the colonel called a meeting of all ranks of Tac. We were gathered at a carefully-selected spot in the woods and there the colonel, unfolding a large map of Normandy, gave us details of the 'scheme'.

At 2 a.m. I awoke with my eyes streaming. Resenting the bad luck which seemed to have burdened me with a head-cold on the eve of the most exciting adventure of my life, I did not realise at first that the tent was on fire and full of smoke.The cause of the fire turned out to be a cigarette end left to burn itself out on the wooden floor of the tent. We hastily extinguished the fire in time for early reveille at 2.15, swallowed a hurried breakfast at 2.45, handed in palliasses and blankets at 3.15, and packed and buckled on our kit, ready to mount the lorries which were to take us to the sea and the waiting LSTs (Landing Ships, Tanks). Tac was to be accommodated in three LSTs, nos. 377, 378 and 379, and was so divided that it could still operate, even if the two of the ships were sunk. On arrival at the ships I gave all my attention to the identities of the passengers and was one of the last to go aboard. The ship's crew were American and the Stars and Stripes fluttered at the masthead between our two barrage balloons.

D-Day had been fixed for 5 June but the inclement weather pinned us to the harbour for the whole of that day. When our party with all its transport was safely aboard the three ships we were at liberty to gaze in wonder upon the sea crowded with shipping and at the sky dotted with barrage balloons. For the greater part of that day an amplifier on deck relayed dance music interrupted at intervals by special announcements or items of news. One of the 'interruptions' was a message from General Eisenhower. Another was the news of the capture of Rome. The voice would stop, and be followed immediately by the throbbing of 'Cow cow Boogie', a tune which is now forever associated in my mind with D-Day. Over all our activities on that first day on the water, whether eating the unaccustomed delicacies of American Army rations – rich beef stew, macaroni and ground rice with hot black coffee – or chatting with the American sailors who described their ship's adventures at Anzio and Salerno, or merely looking incredulously at that fleet of Armageddon, there was an electric, buoyant atmosphere of hushed excitement – like the suspense in the darkening theatre before the rise of the curtain.

At approximately midnight on 5 June, while lying on my bunk, I suddenly felt the vibration of the ship's engines and knew that we were bound for France at last.

Rising early on 6 June I realised I had not a moment to lose. Rolling out of my bunk as speedily as my aching head and querulous stomach would allow, I was soon on the deck leaning over the ship's side in an attitude of careless abandon. Many times on that historic 6 June I repeated this undignified performance, but the general excitement triumphed over temporary bouts of nausea, however numerous. We were now in the open sea, if 'open' is the correct term for that moving landscape bristling with masts as far as the eye could see. Other ships passed us, with their khaki-clad passengers waving or making rude signs as they overtook us. I thought of earlier days and Sunday school treats when bus loads of children behaved in the same way to their rivals on the road. But this was to be no Sunday school treat for those who passed us. They would be there before us and our envy at being overtaken was mixed with pity. Aircraft flew over us in a never-ending stream. It seemed incredible that there could be so many ships or planes in the world. The peak of excitement was reached at approximately 5.30 p.m. as the coast of France came into view.

It was while we had this sight of France still fresh before us that the voice of General Montgomery came through the loudspeakers and we heard him wish us luck. We did not land that day and as soon as darkness fell the all-too-familiar drone of German bombers was heard. Immediately the whole scene was jerked into life by the din of gunfire and continuous streams of tracers. We were ordered below decks when the rain of shrapnel became too heavy, but some of us preferred to stay above rather than miss such a breathtaking sight. It seemed as if every gun on every ship were spitting red balls of fire at the German raiders, and there was one moment when, with an enemy plane directly above us, we seemed to be underneath a huge tent of moving red beads. I was fascinated and almost hypnotised as I sheltered under the bridge with a group of equally excited companions to watch the sparks flying from the iron deck as the falling shrapnel struck against it. Suddenly the air seemed to be sucked away and next a cascade of water splashed upon the deck as a bomb exploded to one side of our ship. It was only a few moments after this when a ship in front of us sustained a direct hit and started to burn furiously. Seeing the casualties from that stricken ship taken aboard our own vessel was our first real taste of war at sea.

There was no sleep for us that night, and all the next day as the Germans were rushing frantic reinforcements to the Normandy coast and the Allies were crowding in to land, we watched the naval shelling and aerial bombardment of the beaches. Almost simultaneously with each flash from a ship's gun a mounting column of smoke reared itself above the seafront, to be followed by a deafening roar. At the same time a never-ending ribbon of aircraft streamed across the Channel to drop their bombs on that small corner of France which only a few hours before had been wrapped in a rural peace. It was hard to imagine what the thoughts and feelings of the surviving inhabitants of those seaside houses must be after four years of quiet remoteness from the sounds of war, to be so violently plunged into the very heart of the conflict.

Punctuating the general din and fury of battle were the sudden, irregular explosions of mines as flail tanks with their gyrating chains cleared a path across the beaches. The sight of our armada, thronging the seascape, and now coming ever closer to land, impressed upon me the thought that I would probably not see so many ships together again. Was there ever such an invasion as this? The whole of that afternoon and evening was spent waiting for the floating platforms called rhinos to take off our heavy vehicles, and it was not until urgent, conflicting demands for priority made by Canadian Army HQ and Tac HQ were shouted through the Tan amplifiers, that we saw the huge steel raft approaching to receive the first of our lorries and armoured cars. During this hazardous operation, undertaken at dusk on 7 June, one of our three-ton trucks with fourteen men and kit belonging to the officers' and sergeants' messes slid off the ramp and disappeared into the sea. The men managed to scramble to safety though they lost all their kit. Much of the mess gear was recovered later. The last of our LSTs disembarked directly on to the beach in the middle of a heavy air raid at 1 a.m. on 8 June.

From the back of the three-ton lorry in which I was sitting uncomfortably on various items of equipment, I had my first glimpse of the Normandy beaches. Death was all around us, imbuing the air we breathed. Though darkness covered the agonies of the previous two days' fighting, a feeling of horror was ever-present. It was the sense of smell which had most to record from those first impressions, added to the gruesome sight of corpses, human and animal.

A shadowy line of German prisoners under escort picked its way along the dusty road, at the sides of which German signs bearing a skull and crossbones hung near the newly erected British notices proclaiming 'Verges not cleared', or 'Verges cleared to 6 ft' giving warning of the presence or absence of mines. Our convoy moved on in the dim half-light while tracer bullets still enlivened the sky with their gay and incongruous fireworks. Only the word PAPETERIE in faded lettering above a shop showed that we were in France and not in a nightmare world. As dawn brightened we moved from that dusty road of phantom trees and anonymous hamlets into the fields where we pitched our first camp.

It was here, while we were lying down for a brief respite under a tree, that one of our men next to me let out a scream. He had received a bullet through the fleshy part of his nose. It came suddenly, mysteriously, unannounced and unaccompanied by others, and at once gave rise to the belief that there were snipers about. This was easily credited as we had just passed the corpse of a German sharp-shooter hanging hideously from a tree in a nearby lane. Another theory, propounded by someone whose commonsense outweighed our nervousness, was that a member of a neighbouring British unit had fired in error on hearing our approach. The mystery was never solved. Fortunately my companion survived after being taken away for prompt treatment to his face.

None of us could escape the feeling of doom which seemed to hang over that field. True, it had been occupied only shortly before our arrival by German troops, a fact to which the many expertly constructed dug-outs bore witness, and there were corpses of cows lying about as evidence of the recent struggle, but the appearance of the field itself was not sufficient to explain our unease. This feeling gained ground among the officers responsible for choosing our camp sites, and no sooner had all our vehicles assembled than arrangements were being made to move off again. Before our departure for the next location I had made some acquaintance with the village and its shocked inhabitants in the cause of security. In such a small headquarters where each member was busy with his own particular job this was something which I had to do on my own. Men, women and children were out in the street to catch sight of their liberators; we were then officially called the BLA, British Liberation Army. While on my lonely search of barns, haylofts and farm buildings for possible German stragglers, I was joined by an enthusiastic young Frenchman whose bicycle had been stolen by the retreating *boches*. There were no extremes to which he would not go for the sake of revenge, and our scrutiny was most thorough.

It was a morning of mingled bewilderment and apprehension, spent in trying to reconnoitre this first battered village with the help of those people who unrestrainedly volunteered their own fragments of information about the startled, retreating enemy while giving me free access to their homes, their attics and cellars, industriously combing through haystacks, heaps of straw and other likely and unlikely hiding places. Reports of snipers in the local countryside were rife, the general opinion being that these were isolated stragglers left behind in the hurried withdrawal of the German troops. Stunned by the noise and confusion of the recent battle, the villagers poured out their anxieties about snipers, looting, and the wholesale destruction of their property, either by the crazed, panic-stricken Germans, or by the overwhelming war machine of the 'liberators'. At the sight of so much endlessly advancing *matériel*, they stood by in attitudes of mixed admiration and wariness. Some were exuberant in their reception of the Allies, others were more guarded: 'Suppose the *boches* were to return and put this invasion into reverse?'

This was a community tired out by four years of German occupation, restrictions, privations and compulsory labour, almost in despair at having to wait so long for the armies of liberation, but nevertheless rejoicing in the prospect of better times to come. They had always clung to the hope that the Allies would come, in spite of the fact that for the last two months the Germans had deprived them of all wireless sets, and told them that British and American bombs were a sufficient proof that the French had been deserted by their friends. There were indications, in the quantities of equipment left behind, and in the almost complete absence of booby-traps in this neighbourhood, that it was the Germans and not the French who were taken in by this propaganda.

Local opinion was unanimous in affirming that the Germans were taken completely by surprise on D-Day. Considering their own wretched plight, the inhabitants of this village were embarrassingly hospitable. I was invited to take note of everything: their inadequate air raid shelters and the fine German ones, their bomb damage, their patched clothes, coarse bread and burnt corn coffee, and the scabs on the faces of babies as a result of lack of milk. Some accepted the Allied bombs as necessary for their liberation. Others who had suffered the loss of home and relatives were embittered by the bombing though still anxious for Allied victory. German morale was described as being extremely low. Strict discipline, the cruelty of commanding officers, and the servility of the average German soldier seemed, in the opinion of the French, all that kept the army together. The villagers reported that when the British troops landed, the German Kommandant in their village was shot by one of his own men.

At 1.30 p.m. I moved off with the reconnaissance party, a skeleton staff of about six men representing transport, defence, signals and operations personnel, to the new site, the park of the Château de Creullet at Cruelly. I interviewed the owners, a retired colonel and his wife, descendants of the old French nobility, who were allowed to remain in residence. A list of names of permanent residents and employees on the estate was obtained from them, and actually only comprised the proprietors, an aged gardener and five other regular employees who came from the village.

I made out passes for these eight people and gave a list of their names together with a specimen pass to the Colonel G (Ops), to the Camp Commandant, to the Officer Commanding Military Police at Tac HQ, and to the OC Defence Company. Before issuing the passes I went to the *mairie*, the office of the mayor, to check up on the character and reliability of the civilians concerned. The mayor was a prisoner in Germany, so I went to the *gendarmerie*. The *gendarmes* of this village had enjoyed a reputation for trustworthiness during the years of occupation and as I was the only Intelligence Corps representative I had to rely on local informants. They had cooperated with the local inhabitants in deceiving the Germans, helped the local youth to dodge slave labour in Germany, and gave assistance to French patriots in hiding. This information was given to me, not by the *gendarmes* themselves but by numerous inhabitants of at least three villages. As a result of my visit to the *gendarmerie* it appeared that all the civilians to whom passes had been made out were inhabitants of long standing, good citizens, and of no danger from a security point of view.

On my return I warned the lady of the château that she must keep all shutters overlooking the caravans closed. This was done forthwith. It was now 9.15 p.m. and at the invitation of the Major G (Ops) I attended a conference at our newly established Creully camp on the defence of Tac HQ. The problem was that, situated as we were in a large park with several entrances and an extensive perimeter, it was difficult not only to control but even, at times, to be aware of unlawful entry. The number of guards and sentries in our small headquarters was naturally limited and we did not use barbed wire or other physical obstacles; so, as I had learnt at Dundee, the best kind of security was provided, not by material defences, but by the quality and vigilance of human beings. The problem therefore centred upon the most effective use of personnel. As a result of this discussion I later, during a stand-to, accompanied officers on a tour of inspection of the defence layout, to decide upon the positioning of the tank and the armoured cars, the placing of sentries, the patrolling by guards, and the most efficient methods of ensuring the security of the perimeter – always, of course, with the safety and survival of our vital Chief in mind.

DUTIES

If I had ever felt guilty during the apparent inactivity of the 'phoney war', the endless preparations for an attack which never seemed to come, the tedious exercises, the boredom, the physical and mental chores, the incongruous entertainments and trivialities on the very brink of universal bloodshed, my conscience found relief in the realisation that I was now in France, overwhelmed by duties which kept me on the run day and night. Meals and sleep were forgotten in the struggle to carry the solitary burden of the security of a top-level headquarters in a time of total war. Added to this official function were the innumerable demands made upon someone known to speak French and German. There were the obvious tasks of counter-intelligence and counter-sabotage for which I had been trained: supervising the physical defences of the camp and its perimeter, cooperating with the Defence Company officers, guards and sentries, and with the Military Police, both British and American, acting as an intelligence link with other intelligence units and writing reports both for Tac HQ and for my superior officer in London. Other duties directly connected with security involved going on detachment on some lone mission away from Tac HQ and contacting front line troops to pick up information about groups or individuals who might prove troublesome to the person of the C-in-C or to the smooth functioning of the headquarters: collaborators, saboteurs and other Nazi or Fascist sympathisers reported to us by forward Intelligence Sections or by civilians. I was also called upon to cooperate in arranging new sites in advanced positions, to explore the ground ahead in readiness for Tac's next move, to investigate rumours, hunt for Germans in hiding on the basis of local gossip, and chase across fields after suspicious-looking pigeons and parachutes. There were also the unexciting routines of checking black-outs both civilian and military, going through innumerable German documents and destroying our own 'secret waste' left behind after a move by a careless or preoccupied clerk.

By far the most interesting part of this unique and sometimes lonely job (lonely because unique) was contact with the civilian population and the wealth and variety of relationships this involved. In many towns and villages through which we passed I was the first British soldier to meet the local resistance movement, and was immediately immersed in a strange mixture of experiences: sad, tragic, happy, exciting, socially warm and friendly, sometimes frightening and at times bordering on the criminal. The tragedies included the disappearance of close relations, and husbands being forcibly separated from their wives, some being sent to forced labour in Germany, others to 'correction' camps about which little was yet known. All these encounters meant the writing of more reports, some of which read more like a novel (or what would now be a television script) than a factual report, which is what they were.

Speaking French left me open to exploitation by those who wanted to supplement their army rations with French cheese, eggs, cream and fresh vegetables. Not that I had any cause for feeling superior, however, as my work with the local population brought me many unsolicited rewards in the form of invitations to supper and occasional eggs for breakfast. At one Normandy farm I was invited to dinner and told to bring a friend. We sat at a long, rough wooden table on benches on the bare stone floor. Meat was turning on a spit in the large open fireplace over a blazing fire, a strange sight for English eyes in the month of June. Neighbours also joined in the meal and conversation was lively and sustained in the convivial French tradition.

Though I was not an official interpreter I was used as one by many of those from whom I had to take orders: deciphering letters written in French or German to General Montgomery by admiring or suppliant locals, arranging a reception for Mabel the cow (a later arrival) which joined the ever-growing menagerie of animals, birds and fish at Tac HQ and the only female ever to be allowed inside the perimeter. Among Monty's four-legged, finned, and feathered friends who lived at Tac to give him comfort and companionship, Mabel was the only one to serve a useful purpose: to provide the Chief with regular supplies of fresh milk. In France I became known among the local population as *l'interprète*, and in Germany as *der Dolmetscher*, my official rôle being much too subterranean and recondite for general publicity. Being used as an interpreter was something I could very often have done without, though there were compensations.

There were a few formal occasions, high level conferences and VIP visits, when all dogsbody jobs had to be abandoned in the interests of increased attention to security. All visitors had to be rigorously scrutinised and their documents checked. This included not only genuine as well as dubious members of the Resistance, but such exalted figures as General Eisenhower, General Bradley, General de Gaulle and Winston Churchill. The latter were usually preceded by groups of war correspondents (among these were personalities familiar to wartime Britain: Richard Dimbleby, Frank Gillard, Alan Moorehead and Chester Wilmot), all of whom had to be carefully vetted, especially as their uniforms had an unfamiliar look to one accustomed to military protocol. Only one person was allowed into the headquarters without being stopped. That was His Majesty King George VI.

There were a number of unpleasant jobs inevitably associated with security. These included dealing with denunciations of suspected traitors and collaborators, with betrayals of whole families by neighbours, and with the mysterious disappearance of various items of property from the headquarters, suspicion of course pointing to the few civilians who had been given passes. Predictably it was nearly always food that was stolen and as we advanced into the hungrier parts of France the looting, if such it could be called, extended to the contents of our dustbins and pigswill.

One of my more frightening experiences was an encounter with a rough, sinister character called H28. Fully acquainted with the news of D-Day and the *débarquement* (landing) on the coast of Normandy, he had somehow made his way from his native Marseille to the north of France to intensify his own work of resistance. He had a powerful physique, short and thick-set, and his face was weather-beaten with a dark growth of stubble. His gravelly voice betrayed his Marseille origin, pronouncing *in* for *en*, for example *in Frince* rather than *en France*.

It was he who introduced me to a branch of the resistance movement at the back of a bicycle shop in Bayeux. Here in conspiratorial closeness I was told that I was the first British soldier they had spoken to, and to celebrate the occasion I was given my first memorable drink of the fiery Calvados. Disregarding the fear expressed by some of their Norman neighbours of a German counter-attack and the need for caution, they showed me how they identified members fo the Resistance in their sector during the occupation. The use of a password, changed at frequent intervals, was accompanied by the fingering of a safety pin hidden in a certain part of the member's clothing. H28 was proud of the number of German soldiers he claimed to have killed, and showed me the weapon with which death had been silently inflicted: a stiletto made from a sharpened knitting needle. He arranged 'dates' for Germans with girls and then when his victim was suitably and vulnerably preoccupied, entered quietly upon the scene with his grisly weapon. As the risks of reprisals were ever-present extreme care was taken to dispose of the bodies and none were found. True or false? It was hard to know, but it was at

times like these, and there were many of them in the course
of wartime duties, that I used to wonder, 'Why am I here?'
'What am I doing?' 'Why am I talking to this man?' 'What
have we in common?' The answer always came back, 'You
are in a war. These are your allies and those are your
enemies. This is what you have in common. Now get on
with it.' The many pressing duties of the moment (for a
soldier, 'set under authority', 'Go and he goeth', 'Do this,
and he doeth it') usually kept other uncomfortable thoughts
at bay, those which had been absorbed many years ago as a
child at my mother's knee and in Sunday school about other
ways of dealing with enemies.

H28 arranged to meet me after dark at a lonely map
reference in a quiet corner of the woods surrounding the
Château of Creullet, for a round-up of collaborators. These
were people, he assured me, who had spent the war years
working for the oppressors of France. *Ces sont des salauds*
(scum). No language could do justice to the enormity of
their crimes. We were to descend upon them at night and
take them by surprise. In the eerie darkness I made out his
small stocky figure then, with him seated behind me on the
pillion of my motor bike, we set off on our nocturnal raid of
traitors' houses, many of them deep in the country. There
were muddy lanes and rutted unmade side roads to be
negotiated in unfamiliar territory and it was difficult,
especially with my blacked-out headlamp, to distinguish any
turning when H28 hissed *à gauche* or *à droite*.

In my training I had been given careful instruction on
house-entering and body-search, but all of this was ignored
by H28. On our arrival at a suspect house he burst in
without warning, merely putting his weight against a door.

The confrontation with the collaborators was terrifying,
for them and for me, but not for H28 who was presumably
getting his revenge upon those who during the long years of
occupation had been enjoying privileges and comforts
unknown to the rest. In this disagreeable drama I was cast
in the uncongenial rôle of witness for the prosecution-cum-

policeman, with H28 as the Grand Inquisitor. He strode into the kitchen, raided the larder: 'How did you come by all this food?' snatching at their smart clothing;

'Traîtres', he yelled.

The men of the household pleaded and wept, and the women, some prostrate, crawling towards me on their knees, plucked at my uniform and clung to me professing their innocence.

'Nous ne sommes pas de traîtres.' (We are not traitors.) 'Ayez pitié monsieur (have pity), bon monsieur, gentil monsieur, ayez pitié. Cher ami ayez pitié.'

This scene was repeated a number of times on that dreadful night as the two of us broke in upon unsuspecting households. The thought that these families, some of them ostensibly wealthy, had played traitor and cheated their poorer neighbours, did not make me feel any happier about that night's work. But who are we to judge? We never had to endure the agonies of occupation, the terrors, the intimidations and the temptations. How would we have behaved?

My overriding worry was that officially I had sole responsibility for the security of Tac Headquarters. I was new to the job and here were people living only a mile or two from the C-in-C of the Allied Land Forces in northwest Europe. What damage could they do if they were truly interested in assisting the enemy? I went giddy at the thought. The houses of those wretched families were placed under surveillance and it came to light that their misdeeds, being crimes against their own French neighbours and without military significance, were no business of the British Army but rather the responsibility of French justices. They were therefore handed over to the *gendarmerie* for judicial investigation. We were constantly on the move and it was tantalising to be in at the beginning of a human story and not at the end.

At a highly mobile stage of the war, and not being qualified to assess the degree of guilt of those hapless victims of a nation's wrath, I was soon called away to other scenes of misery, caused again by people taking the law into their own hands. It was as an observer that I witnessed the fate of others accused (rightly or wrongly) of similar crimes. I was sickened to see women with their heads shaved to the bone, dragged in carts like the tumbrils of the French Revolution through streets and public squares to the jeers of their neighbours. These were women who were known to have had affairs with German soldiers. I found myself asking, 'What sort of world is this?' but this thought had to be quickly stifled by another question, 'Whose side am I supposed to be on?' The very nature of my job demanded cooperation with the Resistance. (It did not, however, in every case demand acquiescence to their methods.)

3

CAMPING IN NORMANDY

Though it was strictly forbidden for troops on active service to keep a diary, one of my continuous duties was to maintain a detailed record of all visitors to the Headquarters and give as accurate an account as possible of the security picture at Tactical Headquarters 21st Army Group. It meant writing secret notes which I kept in a kind of home-made code, and these (labelled SECRET or TOP SECRET) formed the basis of my fortnightly reports to my Commanding Officer, Captain Michael Pertwee (the playwright), at Main Headquarters, then in London. Many of these secrets now appear harmless, from a distance of more than forty years, but though they are interlaced with some of the duller routines of army life and couched in the military jargon of the time I can still recapture, when reading my journal, the obscure drama of many hapless human beings entangled in the miseries of war and the cruelties of enemy occupation.

Visitors to our camp included the lawful and the unlawful. In the first category were those who carried *and showed* the authorised pass accompanied by proof of identity. One of my regular chores was to issue passes to civilians vetted as workers permitted to pass through the camp boundaries and the supervise the checking of identities by the sentries and Military Police on duty at the entrance. It was while we were at Creully that I came unexpectedly to appreciate my training, especially my power station masquerades, when I was urgently called to the camp entrance. There the sentry on duty, wholesomely aware of his responsibility, was standing with a fixed bayonet confronting a towering, outraged French officer who kept repeating:

'Mais je suis le Général de Gaulle.'

He was reluctant to show proof of identity. In an effort to support the sentry in his task I asked the visitor for his *carte d'identité* but he was still unwilling to comply. It has to be said that such an occurrence was strangely at odds with the usual protocol, which ensured that when a VIP (an abbreviation dating from this time) was expected all defence personnel were alerted. Signals were invariably very quick to establish lines of communication, but on this occasion no message had reached the sentry, for whom this was 'a surprise visit'.

The ultimatum when given was not graciously received:

'Personne n'entre par ici, monsieur, sans identification.' (No one enters here Sir, without identification.)

He was obviously General de Gaulle, but I had learnt that we could never afford to take risks. I remembered that even Winston Churchill was obliged to produce his pass at London conferences and the affable Americans took all such procedures for granted, General Eisenhower putting his hand on my shoulder, handing me his wallet saying:

'Help yourself son.'

This was different. After some pressure and obstinacy on our part the visitor relented at last, showed his *laissez-passer* and was given access to General Montgomery, who when we were reported was quick to spring to our defence. The word soon went round that Monty's guest was told:

'Stop belly-aching. Those men have a job to do.'

The more doubtful callers consisted of all sorts and conditions of men, women and children, from the suspect and potentially dangerous to the miscellaneous. This latter group grew progressively larger as we advanced further into northern France and reached its zenith in Belgium. The work of stemming this rising tide started, however, in a small way in Normandy, where the identity of our chief remained for a few weeks a closely guarded secret. There were genuine as well as dubious members of the Resistance, tale-bearers, rumour-mongers, beggars, refugees and trespassers in the form of tramps, gypsies, strollers and sightseers. Though many of these people were simply nuisances in that they added to an already heavy burden of work, all having to be stopped, searched and questioned, their most serious fault was to divert attention from the determined intruder who might be a spy, saboteur, terrorist or assassin.

Imagine therefore my alarm when at 4 a.m. on 11 June I was awakened by the guard to interrogate a German soldier who had been caught *inside the camp perimeter* and only a few yards from General Montgomery's caravan. So much for security. Interrogation and search were carried out, and articles numbered and labelled. He was aged eighteen, a Sudeten German in the infantry, stationed in the neighbourhood since November. He said he was alone. In the shock and confusion of the D-Day invasion his comrades had left him behind. No one had been giving him food, and owing to a shortage of rations he had given himself up. He had been hiding in a hole in the depths of some rhododendron bushes in the vicinity of the château for three days and was very scared and hungry. As this frightened adolescent with trembling fingers emptied his pockets of his few possessions, including a photograph of his mother, we were given a view of the German army quite different from the one publicised by our news media. After being offered food and the inevitable mug of tea, which he regarded with distrust until I drank form it, our prisoner was kept under guard until daylight. He was then re-examined by the Military Police and taken by a sergeant and two men of the Defence Company to POW Cage 50 Div.

When considering this breach of security, we might say that he had not penetrated the British Army but that the British Army had encircled him. But from then on no thicket, shrubbery or spinney within our camp boundary escaped the closest scrutiny. It meant literally beating the bushes, leaving no stone unturned, looking for needles in haystacks, peering into every hole and corner. After this shock revelation of the enemy within our gates every conceivably unusual event was reported to me, and at all hours of the day and night. Nervous sentries were particularly alerted whenever passers-by showed more than ordinary curiosity about the British presence. At night these civilians were referred to not as strollers but as prowlers, and from there it was but a short step to suspects, then spies and saboteurs. The villagers, subjected to strict surveillance for four years, fell an easy prey to spy mania, and called regularly at the camp with stories of treacherous neighbours and suspicious strangers. I was therefore kept busy.

At 11.30 p.m. one night, in pouring rain, the military policeman on duty came to my tent, opened the flap, shone his half blacked-out torch and reported:

'I've got my doubts about two characters I caught lurking about the gate. They wanted to know a bit too much, who we were, where we were from and where we are going. A bit stupid, I reckon, but you can't be too careful, especially at this hour of the night. If you come now we can get them.'

In confirmation of his suspicions he described them as having flaxen hair, jack-boots and military-style clothing.

We went in search of them and with the help of local residents who were also concerned about the presence of these strangers among them, we found them in the village café. From my conversation with them it appeared that the two young men were evacuees:

'We are French. Before the *débarquement*, we were in the German labour call-up. With all the fighting and the bombing and the German retreat we ran away too. So here we are.'

Their papers were in order and there was nothing fishy except the flaxen hair and the jackboots. Experience should have taught me that not all blonds are Germans, nor are the French exclusively brunette.

One nocturnal expedition did, however, lead to an arrest. I was again called out at a late hour to investigate a suspect. He was reported to us by a group of local inhabitants whose suspicions had been aroused when he applied for work in the town and refused to produce his identity card on demand. He sought lodging for the night with Monsieur Winkel, a sawyer, who was so disturbed by the elusive behaviour and foreign accent of his visitor that he quietly went out and reported his anxieties to the officer in charge of our Armoured Car Troop at one of the entrances to the château. I went with this officer and an armed guard to the house where Monsieur Winkel was waiting to speak to us:

'Il est tout à fait suspect. C'est un étranger dans notre village, et il parle avec un accent. Vous le trouverez en haut, au lit.' (He is a thoroughly suspicious character, a stranger in our village, and talks with an accent. You'll find him upstairs in bed.)

We climbed the stairs and took the lodger by surprise. While getting dressed he offered this explanation:

'I was conscripted for the Todt Organisation (German Labour Force) to erect defences at Cherbourg, but I left there because of the heavy bombing. I was making my way to Caen, and got as far as Creully where I asked for lodging at the house of Monsieur Winkel.'

'How did you expect to get into Caen through the German lines?'

'I thought Caen had been captured' (he did not say 'liberated') by the Allies. I have walked all the way from Cherbourg spending nights sleeping in barns and hedges.'

The recent rain had probably driven him to seek shelter indoors. In spite of my previous reservations I had to observe that he was fair-haired and not French-looking. He appeared well-fed and did indeed speak French with a peculiar accent. When I asked him to show me his papers his answers were guarded. He possessed one identity card, blue in colour, unlike the light brown card issued to French civilians. He was nineteen and of Czech nationality.

With many lingering doubts about this man's truthfulness we escorted him to the headquarters of V Corps US Army where we were introduced to an officer of Combat

Intelligence who said that the suspect would be housed and fed there that night and interrogated next morning by Counter-Intelligence personnel. We left V Corps at 2 a.m. At 2.30 a.m. I reported the night's proceedings to the officer commanding Defence Company.

Though our camp was comparatively small with its tight cluster of tents and caravans, it was scattered, largely because the chief insisted on living in seclusion, sometimes in a separate field. This meant that, with our limited number of military police and defence troops, the entire perimeter of park or farm could not be guarded at any one time. Sentries were posted at strategic points, there were regular patrols of the boundary and a tank and armoured car guarded the carefully concealed approaches to the Chief's caravans. There were therefore gaps in our physical defences through which the occasional unsuspecting strangers could penetrate. They then had to be treated as trespassers and interrogated. In France their numbers were controllable, but in liberation-crazed Belgium they were to be a permanent headache.

In Normandy some people came to the camp with the deliberate purpose of denouncing a suspected collaborator or, for example, a neighbour known to come from Alsace. One man reported that the grass in a nearby field was being cut in the shape of an arrow pointing directly at our headquarters. Other visitors found themselves inside our perimeter, as much to their own surprise as to ours. A one-legged soldier from the Foyer des Invalides at Villiers-le-Sec was found walking in the park of Creullet and had to be questioned. He explained that the people of the château had always allowed the wounded soldiers from the hospital to take their recreation in the park. This old man was enjoying his usual walk and did not know that, since the recent D-Day landings, entry to the grounds was now prohibited to civilians. He did not seem to be aware that he had just been liberated.

One afternoon I saw a woman with a crowd of children walking through the camp. She was Madame Jacqueline

Ménage and was begging for food at the cookhouse. She was born in Jersey where, she said, she had been engaged to an Englishman who was killed in the war. She later moved to Cherbourg and was a refugee from that town. I told her that the camp was barred to civilians, and she must not come again. Her parting shot can only be expressed in French: 'Les Anglais et les Américains, ce sont ma vie. Je m'appelle Jacqueline Ménage. Appelez-moi Jacky et vous pouvez oublier le ménage.'*

In retrospect it seems incredible now that unauthorised persons should find themselves even unknowingly so close to such a sensitive centre of wartime operations. It was typical of General Montgomery that the security of his Tactical Headquarters depended not on rolls of barbed wire and intricate fortifications but on the vigilance of the men whose duty it was to guard him. Apart from the young German soldier driven into hiding by the disorder of retreat, no trespassers got very far. Such was the character of the landscape in which we usually camped, and so mobile was the headquarters (here today and gone tomorrow), that our boundaries were defined not so much by impregnable barriers as by patrolling guards always on the watch.

Daily and nightly patrols of the camp perimeter and the village were part of my own routine. This included entering houses whose windows overlooked our site, though we were usually so secluded that the duty did not often arise. Civilians who had to travel through our boundaries on their way to work in château or farm were careful to show their passes. One of these workers was a fifteen-year-old maidservant who lived in Creully and had been known to the owners of the property from childhood. By a peculiar coincidence I came upon her again in 1981 in Caen when I chanced to spend a night in a hotel of which she was the proprietress. Reminiscing about the war brought to light the fact that we had met before.

---

* The English and the Americans, they are my life. My name is Jacqueline Ménage. Call me Jacky and you can forget about the ménage.

There were times when security required me to stay in the headquarters for conferences, for visits by VIPs or reporters or entertainers such as 'Stars in Battledress' or George Formby, or a morning spent sorting out German papers ready for disposal by Military Intelligence (Ia). On this last occasion I kept guard over the room containing the German documents while the owners of the château removed glass and chinaware. There was a vast quantity of boxes left intact, presumably as there had been no time to destroy or dispose of anything during the sudden onslaught of the D-Day landings. The retreating Seventh Grenadier Regiment had left behind their Battle Orders, papers marked GEHEIM (Secret), others 'For Service Use Only', marked maps, diaries, letters, rubber stamps, identity discs, manuals on the British, French, American and Russian armies, diagrams of our ships, photographs and private possessions, in addition to 2,000 francs and odd change. This money was put in the care of G (Ops).

It was while I was working in this room that an officer from Monty's inner circle arrived with a request for a chamber pot for the C-in-C. After some initial misunderstanding with a baffled Madame de Druval, the elderly chatelaine offering an unlikely collection of flower vases, the required object was produced amidst chuckles on both sides. This event finally succeeded in breaking any ice still existing between our involuntary hosts and ourselves.

Although I enjoyed the companionship and friendliness of my fellow comrades in rare moments of leisure at the camp, my duties often took me away on solitary journeys to investigate wild stories of Germans in hiding, of collaborators in disguise, of potential spies and saboteurs in woods or secluded outhouses, as well as verifiable accounts of hidden stocks of German food and piles of jettisoned documents, ammunition, weapons and live grenades. These travels involved detailed reports and further excursions to the appropriate military authorities to dispose of the material, for example the removal by the Royal Engineers of possible booby-traps left in burnt-out German vehicles on the Paris–Cherbourg road, or the collection and deciphering by Signals staff of German papers. Some were lonely visits, but others were in the company of a Military Policeman or Defence Company Officer to 'suspect' houses and isolated farm buildings. Some jobs required the presence of a witness who also served as armed protection, as in the interrogation of an enemy prisoner or the rounding up of snipers in a church, or the investigation of flashing lights and rifle shots at night. Air raids formed a regular background to these nocturnal outings. One of these scored a direct hit on one of the tents in our Creully camp, killing one man, injuring others and destroying property.

One alarming exception to the reassuring presence of an escort was the occasion when, walking alone through a wood in broad daylight about a mile from the camp, I saw two men on the same path walking towards me. They were wearing uniform and as they came nearer I saw that they were German soldiers. Reaching for my revolver I had no alternative but to continue walking, though I must confess that I began to sweat and to hold my breath. We kept on coming closer to each other so that their pale, unshaven faces were quite clear. Then to my intense relief one of them took a white handkerchief out of his pocket and raised it above his head. I motioned them with my revolver to walk in front of me and marched them back to the camp where an astonished police guard received them and then drove them, with me, to the nearest POW cage.

A regular exercise throughout the campaign was reconnaissance of new sites for the headquarters, sometimes alone on my motor bike, and sometimes with a sergeant or officer of the Military Police. This involved checks on the local population, usually with the assistance of the *gendarmerie* and recommended prominent citizens who might be the mayor, the priest or the school teacher. Our next camp site after Creully was a farm in the village of Blay, near Bayeux, midway between the British and American armies. We were in for a long stay here while the battles of Caen and the Cherbourg Peninsula were fought.

FRIENDS IN THE VILLAGE

Soon after our arrival in Blay the colonel, who was sensitive both to the feelings of the French and to our need for their cooperation, sent for me and gave instructions that from now on all official communication with the local population must be made through me. It was essential to secure their goodwill as many of our operational requirements would appear to militate against this. Every effort was made to build positive relationships with our neighbours; this proved to be the most enjoyable and rewarding aspect of my work, if work it could be called. It was officially known as security but to me it really meant making friends (an enterprise that has borne fruit in friendships lasting to the present day).

It has to be said that our efforts to secure friendly public relations with the villagers of Blay were essential as in the early days of our prolonged sojourn our contact with them began to seem uncomfortably like the treatment meted out to a subject race by their oppressors: orders to fell trees for the building of Monty's private airstrip, the removal of cows from this airfield once it had been constructed, arrangements to widen gates and demolish hedges to allow passage for our larger vehicles, the caravans, the Signals and Operations lorries, the tank and the armoured cars, and instructions to the farmer, Monsieur François Hamel, about the use or rather the non-use of his fields during our occupation of them. I told Monsieur and Madame Hamel that passes would be issued to them and that traffic to the farm would be channelled through one entrance only, so that they might have the use of their back garden gate for themselves. I obtained from them a list of people living or working on the farm, and an invitation to dinner which I accepted. I contacted the neighbouring farmer, Monsieur Aumond, and gave him instructions about mowing two fields where the C-in-C was to have his caravans. Naturally, all these directions had to be given without betraying the identity of the camp or its Chief. In spite of these orders and restraints, or even because of them (it emerged later that other farmers became jealous of François Hamel – because of post-war compensation?), all the local inhabitants to whom I spoke in this small, scattered community seemed pleased to see us, especially the children, who offered us flowers. The farmers would be allowed to use most of their fields and to milk their cows, but must carry their passes at all times. The C-in-C's field was out of bounds to all civilians, without exception.

While I was obsessed by my own immediate cares, the man upon whom so many hopes were placed, on whose decisions much of Western civilisation depended, and whose continuing existence was the point of all our efforts at security, moved quietly in and out of his isolated headquarters almost unnoticed through his own private entrance leading to the seclusion of an empty field and his carefully camouflaged den, the three caravans. It was a long time, therefore, before the villagers of Blay, his own immediate neighbours, discovered the identity of the mysterious occupant of these pastures.

It was during one of my tours of the village that I heard some shrewd guesses being made by local inhabitants about the identity of their famous neighbour. They had noticed that the camp was too well-guarded for an ordinary formation. They were all too aware of the presence of tanks and armoured cars at strategic points. They had seen barriers across roads labelled *Défense d'entrer*, and their movements had been restricted by barred fields. Their curiosity had been aroused by lorries which served as offices and others used as wireless stations, but above all by the aeroplane which was neither fighter nor bomber. They had also observed that we were the only British troops in an area occupied exclusively by Americans. One man remarked that General Montgomery, being in command of both American and British troops, would choose a location midway between the two sectors. Most convincingly of all, the C-in-C had been seen in the vicinity and had been recognised from photographs on RAF leaflets.

My routine duties were interrupted by other events at Tac HQ which should have betrayed the presence of its principal character. These involved ceremonial, protocol and the inevitable vetting of visitors. One important occasion was the Investiture of General Bradley of First US Army on 13 July, attracting crowds of press representatives, among whom were some well-known BBC radio personalities; another was General Montgomery's press conference on 19 July.

With stories and rumours circulating with such abandon throughout the village community, it was remarkable that the farmer and his wife on whose land we were camped, were among the last to suspect the presence of General Montgomery in their corner field. François reported to me on 9 July (the day when Caen fell to the Allies) that one of the workmen laying telephone cables told him that he was going to work at the headquarters (*le quartier général*) in Blay, but he did not believe the rumour that General Montgomery was in Blay. Later Madame Hamel told me that while she was visiting her friend who lived in the cottage at the top of the field in which the G (Ops) caravan was parked, she had been able to watch the investiture though it was too far away for her to be able to recognise faces. She knew something important was happening because she had seen the crowd of press people. Both she and her husband realised that there was someone of very high rank in the camp. Their friends in the village, consumed with curiosity, had hinted that it was General Montgomery, but this they refused to believe.

Monsieur and Madame Hamel were a steady (in both senses of the word) source of information about local events and reactions during and after the German occupation. Monty had his own private means of access to his caravan, away from the house, but one day at last Monsieur and Madame Hamel saw for themselves and recognised in the village not only General Montgomery but Churchill as well.

Monty's cloak of secrecy was to be torn away later when, travelling through the large towns of northern France, he was recognised, and in the feverish excitement of our passage through Brussels he ordered his chauffeur to slow down so that he could acknowledge the cheers of the crowd and enjoy seeing and being seen. These Roman-style triumphal processions were to make life more difficult for those responsible for the Chief's safety. When, in Belgium, our camp was under siege from admirers, well-wishers, gift-bearers and autograph-hunters, I longed for the anonymity of Normandy.

4

IMPRESSIONS AND OPINIONS
IN NORMANDY

O ur long stay in Blay during the battle for Caen meant that a greater warmth and openness developed in our relationships with the local people, especially once it became clear that our bridgehead was established and the danger of a German return had receded. People marvelled at the volume and variety of our *matériel* which, compared with the noticeably declining resources of the Wehrmacht, gave every appearance of being invincible. On the dusty roads of Normandy they gazed in wonderment at the endless convoys of strange vehicles: lorryloads of troops, wireless caravans, ships on wheels (Dukws), tanks that swam and some with massive flails of chain that disposed of mines.

One of the most interesting and friendly characters in the village was the priest, Monsieur Arsène, whom it was my duty to contact in my search to locate churches for Monty's regular church parades. War or no war the Commander-in-Chief insisted on having a service every Sunday. The fact that the church was Roman Catholic made no difference to his requirements. The *curé* had no objections but the Second Army RC Chaplain did. The Church of England worship went ahead in spite of his complaints.

As I was to be the channel through which instructions reached the civilian population it soon became obvious to me that my best opposite number on the French civilian side in Blay was the village priest. He was the most knowledgeable and efficient ambassador for speedy communication of understanding and sympathy between us and the local inhabitants, upon whose cooperation so much of the day-to-day conduct of the war depended. The *curé* was very friendly and obliging, lending me books and music for our church services, and full of advice for the British whom he considered (mistakenly?) to have been too indulgent towards the Germans after the First World War. Monsieur Arsène, a bricklayer's son, was both a quasi-communist and a priest, as well as a man of the people. He was forty-two and had been in the army, a prisoner of war in Germany, but had been repatriated on medical grounds. He had a small nephew whose hobby was collecting RAF and American leaflets which, along with Allied news and propaganda, aimed to give heart to people in the occupied countries. Children in the village used to exchange them as children in England would swap cigarette cards or stamps. It was from photographs printed on these leaflets that French civilians were able to identify our war leaders, among whom Eisenhower and Montgomery were the most prominent. Monty's face and the famous beret were therefore familiar wherever we went.

During my rounds of the village I visited the local café and talked to the people there. They had never imagined that the Allies would land in Normandy, but expected us to invade the Pas de Calais coast. Among the customers in the café were a few men from different parts of France and it was clear from their disparaging remarks that they did not care for country folk in general or Normans in particular. A Parisian workman said that we landed in the worst place for welcome. He remarked that the Norman's only religion was his pocket-book (*son portefeuille*) and that he would sell his produce to a German more readily than to his own countryman because he would be better paid. Another from Paris said that the farmers let the rest of the population down in this way. He was speaking from the painful experience of hunger. Traces of bitterness and resentment were noticeable as the conversation turned towards conditions in Paris, which were very bad. Milk was very scarce, even for babies. Elsewhere in the towns things were not much easier. Butter in Nice was being sold for eighteen hundred francs.

As a member of a country which had experienced the bombs but not the physical presence of the enemy, I could only be a listener during such conversations as this. Who was I to judge between Parisians and Normans? My intervention, if any, could only be that of questioning sympathetically and seeking information. But I did observe, in some of the heated exchanges, how war could divide as well as unite compatriots.

Yet the Normans suffered hardships too. Though we did not observe the severe outward signs of starvation which were later to shock us in Holland, we did see many village children with scabs and drawn faces and other signs of malnutrition. I learnt in conversation with Madame Alix, a farmer's wife, that they had been hard hit by the German occupation. Although the German soldiers did not treat her badly they did strip the farm of cattle, oats and barley. Prices were so high that she found it difficult to feed her six children, four boys and two girls. One boy of fourteen was without shoes and socks, while she had to pay 300 francs for a pair of boots for the three-year-old girl. At Monsieur Le Paulmier's farm I was again told that there was no serious food shortage in the neighbourhood, but conditions in the towns were very bad, especially for children. The food situation in Rouen was described as being worse than in Paris: Paris hotels were known to serve cats to their customers.

As I became better acquainted with people in the village I heard of some of the tragedies resulting from the D-Day onslaught. One man was killed and two women were seriously injured by an American hand-grenade thrown into the trench where they were taking shelter, and there were other cases of people being killed although they took no part in the fighting. The nineteen-year-old daughter of Monsieur and Madame Lamoureux was killed by a bomb on D-Day. Madame Pegouet's brother, her only close relative, was killed by a bomb in Caen. He was a missionary, and an air raid warden, in the *Défense Passive*. The mother of a boy from La Cambe was killed on D-Day, yet he was keen to join up. The mother and twelve-month-old son of a school teacher evacuated from a village in La Manche were killed in an RAF raid. I was told that RAF Mosquitoes came over the village eight times in one day to destroy a railway bridge. The village was wiped out, but the bridge remained. The school master thought that our Bomber Command made a grave psychological error when planning the large-scale bombing raids on France. He recalled an anti-British demonstration by Frenchmen in Paris after a severe raid on Montmartre:

'There has been a lot of unnecessary destruction,' he said, 'but worst of all is Rouen.' (Mais le pire c'est Rouen.)

He had a poor opinion of our accuracy in bombing and said that many towns which had been pro-British had now changed their attitude. He gave Nantes and Cherbourg as examples.

It was natural that my British presence among them was a heaven-sent opportunity to vent pent-up feelings, whether of anger or relief. In a confused way I appreciated the fact that they felt free to express such feelings, and kept silent. Other villagers, perhaps embarrassed by the school teacher's undisguised bitterness, expressed different attitudes. From their point of view the communiqué announcing the capture of Cherbourg was badly worded. Comparison was made between the enthusiastic welcome which greeted the troops in Cherbourg and the *sourires fades* (the insipid smiles) in other parts of Normandy.

Other citizens whom I was privileged to meet were quietly persistent in their patriotic pride, their support for the Allies and their hostility to the Nazis. Following a patrol, accompanied by officers of the Defence Company, we interviewed the manageress of the cheese factory, who was reputed to be enthusiastically pro-British. She was a smart, slim, sophisticated woman, elegantly though simply dressed in typical French fashion. Her fluent command of her own language, in beautifully structured phrases, was devoted mainly to praise of the English and our war effort. The word 'British' appeared not to have gained wide currency among those whom we met on the Continent of Europe.

'J'admire le caractère anglais, en effet up peu comme nous autres Normands, calmes, sensés.' (I admire the English character, in fact a bit like us Normans, calm, sound.) 'Et votre matériel, c'est formidable, éblouissant, incroyable. Avec ça pas moyen de rater la guerre.' (And your equipment, it's fantastic, dazzling, unbelievable. With that it's impossible to lose the war.)

She had conducted a prolonged campaign of insolence against the Germans and set in motion a benevolent black market for the French, most of whom refused to eat the bad cheese ordered for them by the occupying power. It was reported that at the end of a stormy interview one of the Gestapo officers had said to her:

'Madame, you do not love the Germans.'

Whereupon the manageress sent for her papers and, taking her contract out of the file she replied:

'Monsieur, my contract says I am to supply you with cheese, not love.'

This woman also refused to send her employees to erect anti-glider obstacles in the fields. She said that she could not have continued this campaign much longer with impunity, and was only saved from the Gestapo by our invasion. The Nazis stole 150,000 cases of condensed milk from the factory on the Saturday before D-Day.

On another occasion I called at the Horticultural School to see another enthusiastic anglophile, Madame Marcelle Fauchier Delavigne, a great-niece of the poet and dramatist Casimir Delavigne. She was living in the remains of what had once been an eleventh-century monastery, complete with church tower and oubliettes. In a three-hour conversation I learned much about French opinion. There was great local support for General de Gaulle. The Germans were aware of this and one sign of their unease was their distrust of the *gendarmerie*; well-founded, perhaps, as a nephew of the police chief was in the Maquis. In this part of Normandy the inhabitants were struck by the poor morale of the Germans, who openly betrayed their war-weariness; one German soldier on his return from leave was reported as saying, *Vaterland kaput* (The Fatherland is finished). Soldiers in the Trouville district were said to be mostly boys in their teens. (Hitler apparently had not sent his crack troops to Normandy.) Officers in that town invented cruel punishments such as making men walk backwards and forwards on the tips of their toes and fingers without bending their knees. All the French people I met seemed impressed by the smart discipline of the German army but were disgusted by the servility of the average soldier.

The local people were regular listeners to our radio broadcasts and so were *au fait* with our war effort. Though there was enthusiasm for the Allies and hatred of the Nazis they were still distressed by the inevitable devastation of French towns and monuments. They too were of the opinion that the RAF bombing had lost us many friends. Others said:

'On ne fait pas d'omelette sans casser des œufs.'

Increasingly the villagers became as willing to talk as I was to listen, especially to their descriptions of life under the Nazi occupation. Many broke down in tears when recalling their tragic losses and bereavements.

According to three school masters, two of whom were acting mayors, there were four kinds of attitude during the occupation, crudely typified by those who were roughly recognisable as either francophiles, anglophiles, germanophiles or, to coin a word, egophiles.

The first category contained many serious thinkers and intellectuals who had the interests of their country at heart; wanting to be on good terms with the Allies, if only to give France peace, security and a government representative of the people. They were people who had worried and thought about the destiny of France for years under conditions not favourable to risk-taking or spontaneity in international relationships.

While they were realists in their attitude to the governments of the United States and Great Britain, they were still friendly and charming in their relations with the Allied troops. They were openly critical of the see-saw politics of Great Britain in the years between the wars and desired closer cooperation between the democracies after this war.

Though the majority of the French who came in contact with Allied soldiers were friendly, not all were anglophiles. The anglophiles I met seemed to be even more pro-British than the British themselves. They were contemptuous of their own countrymen for their lack of unity and stamina and made flattering comparisons between our war effort and that of the French. I encountered very few people with this outlook and considered the francophiles to be more representative of French opinion. There were many Frenchmen, however, who fell between the two categories and did not regard the terms francophile and anglophile as being incompatible. All the children appeared to be spontaneously and uninhibitedly anglophile in the presence of British soldiers. Although the enthusiasm of the very young might have been due more to a love of *bonbons* and *cigarettes pour papa* than to a love of the Allies, it was plain that the more mature youth of France were sincerely friendly. Several young Frenchmen had tried to join the British and United States Armies and the term anglophile might be said to include Americans, though distinctions were made between US and British troops. American soldiers made a better impression locally on their arrival than the British troops. They were described as being more exuberant, more simple-hearted, and more generous. The English appeared cold and distant but, one Frenchman reassured me, the people of Normandy who are themselves cold and placid, would soon tire of American turbulence, and would be more at home with the calm, sober and less extrovert English.

From the social point of view, as people to converse with and invite into their homes, they preferred the British soldiers, but from the military point of view they expressed more confidence in the Americans. This might have been due to the fact that American convoys passed through the village daily and they had not yet seen much British equipment, or it might be another example of the old prejudices dating back to Dunkirk, the last war and back into time. Monsieur and Madame Hamel were both struck by the degree of equality existing in the American Army between officers and men. They thought some of our older officers, especially the colonel, *très distingués, très gentils, très bien*, and a few of the younger ones arrogant. They seemed fond of the other ranks, without exception, a sentiment no doubt arising from the fact that many of them were nearer their own station in life, were *pères de famille*, far from home and, like themselves, victims of a cruel war. Madame Hamel said that she had got used to the soldiers being about the farm and would miss us if we went. She remarked wistfully that the fields would look strange and empty without the lorries and tents. On the night we were invited to dinner at the farmhouse we were told that there had been repeated sabotage of the railway line between Paris and Cherbourg during the German occupation. The result was that all able-bodied men had to stand guard over the track, each being responsible for a certain distance. One portion in particular was being continually unbolted between Caen and Lisieux. The story goes that the saboteur, when arrested, was discovered to be a German soldier. He said he was tired of the war and the army.

Apart from one German prisoner and one Czech Todt worker who professed love for France. I met no people upon whom the doctrine of Hitlerism had made any but the most painful impression. The minority of people who made themselves comfortable under German rule were, very generally, misguided advantage-seekers, profiteers or prostitutes, with no convinced political or ideological commitment. To the pro-German group belonged the defeatists who thought that France would be better disciplined under the stronger rule of Germany, and so sold their services to Hitler. Among these were a few wealthy political intriguers, quasi-Fascists, social outcasts and international hooligans.

Prostitutes continued in their profession regardless of conscience or consequences; some women fell in love with individual Germans to whom they remained faithful in the teeth of savage reprisals from their neighbours; and some sold themselves simply to survive.

The last category, the 'egophiles', also contained a small minority who were more interested in their personal welfare than in that of the country. They often proved to be rich, bourgeois and owners of large châteaux who did not hesitate to say that the Germans were *très corrects* while tactfully pointing out that our tanks and lorries did not improve the amenities of their parks and gardens.

The most engrossing problem for the French under German rule was shortage of food. The ration of butter was 50 grams per month, and this commodity was more plentiful in Normandy than other essential foodstuffs. The price of butter locally was in the neighbourhood of 60 francs per kilo but it was sold on the Paris black market for 800 francs per kilo. Bread was scarce and of inferior quality; suet and oil were unobtainable; salt had been and still was rare; and eggs and vegetables were requisitioned by the Germans. The French were not allowed to buy vegetables in the shops and had to rely on produce from their gardens. Meat of all kinds was required to feed soldiers on the Russian front. Clothes, furniture and pharmaceutical articles were only for the very rich. Iodine, medicinal alcohol and cotton wool were unobtainable and there were no first-aid preparations for the *Défense Passive* (ARP). One air raid warden was obliged to draw upon a private stock which he had hoarded from the days of peace. Soap was of very poor quality; it did not lather and left a gritty deposit in the bottom of the wash-basin. A toothbrush cost 80 francs, and a pair of spectacles which cost 370 francs before the war, was now 1,050 francs.

Life was particularly hard for children. In French schools only those books consistent with the Nazi ideology were allowed. Though the doctrines of Hitlerism were not preached, all lessons and books in favour of French ideals were strictly forbidden. Periodical inspections were carried out by German officials, and schools were thoroughly searched for subversive literature.

One disturbing symptom of the war in France was the distrust of one Frenchman for another; denunciations for money were commonplace under the German occupation. One Gestapo officer is reported to have said:

'The French make me sick. There are so many letters of denunciation that we have had to open a special office for the purpose and there is not enough staff to deal with all this correspondence.'

One Frenchman, the secretary to a mayor, had to conceal from his neighbours that he was an escaped prisoner from Germany; otherwise, he said, he would certainly have been denounced. This practice still continued in the liberated zone. One enquiring why so many Frenchmen were in the habit of denouncing their fellow countrymen, I was given the following reasons: after the fall of France, which was a moral as well as a military collapse, it seemed as if the French, bewildered and disillusioned, let themselves go. Their morale sank to a very low level and their patriotism suffered. When the Germans came certain French people, more materialistic and unscrupulous than the majority of the population, said to themselves:

'We have lost everything. What more is there to lose? Let's make the most of life, and at the same time make some money.'

These were the people who did not object to favouring the Germans with their attentions and they were well paid for it.

The rest of the population, who were struggling to uphold the remnants of national honour, also said to themselves:

'When the Allies come we shall denounce these people. They must be punished.'

This resulted in the Allied troops beholding the disagreeable spectacle of one Frenchman denouncing another.

It was said that the towns were more patriotic than the countryside. Normandy in particular had enjoyed more abundance than the rest of France and was criticised by Parisians for being somnolent, forgetful and isolationist – the Normans wanted to be left alone. Theirs was the richest province of France and supplied the whole of the country with milk, butter, eggs, cheese, meat, fruit and vegetables. The south of France, for example, could only produce fruit and wine, and in consequence hardship in this region was very great. The Germans favoured agricultural workers and farmers to the detriment of other workers. Those worst off were the employees of factories, artisans, garage-hands, miners and other heavy manual labourers, and it is not surprising that these were said to be the most patriotic sections of the population.

The opinion was often expressed that while the morale of France was low, given a leader who could revive their patriotism the French would rise. Pétain almost achieved this revival by the paternal attitude he initially exhibited, but when his German leanings and compromises became too obvious the people lost hope again. As a future leader of France, de Gaulle was welcomed.

On the night of 14 July (Bastille Day) a friend and I were invited to dinner at the Hamel's farm to celebrate. Our hosts talked about life during the German occupation and also about the Americans who were in the village before us. They admitted that the behaviour of the average German soldier towards civilians was 'correct' as long as things were going well for them, but in retreat they had other things to think about than creating a good impression on the local population. Madame de Druval at the château of Creullet said that the German officers in command of white Russian volunteers (or, more probably, conscripted prisoners) billeted in the lodge immediately prior to our own arrival, were *très corrects*, while she described the conduct of the Russians as 'most ill befitting soldiers of the Czar.'

Nearly every French civilian with whom I spoke had anecdotes to relate concerning Germans who expressed their intention of surrendering 'as soon as the Tommies came', yet on the day of the invasion the Germans did no such thing and fought hard and well. I learnt that in the local café Germans never spoke openly in front of other Germans, but would confide in French civilians when none of their compatriots were present. Some expressed weariness with the Nazi régime; one soldier said that after the war Mamma would be of more importance to him than Hitler. He was going back to her and he did not care if he never heard the name of the Führer again. Others said that their first duty on the day of the invasion would be to kill their commanding officer. This threat materialised at Tour-en-Bessin when a German captain was shot by his own men. This was the second case of this nature that I encountered.

One German entered a village shop and said that when the war was over he was going to join the communists. Another German walked in just in time to hear the word 'communist'. Obviously frightened by being overheard the first German paled but the other stepped forward, grasped him by the hand and said 'Comrade'.

The people of the surrounding villages and towns were unanimous in saying that the German army of the day was very short of essential stores, chiefly food, oil, fats and petrol, and that this was in striking contrast to the condition of the troops who had originally occupied the district. (The war in Russia was obviously taking its toll on Hitler's resources.) German soldiers were said to have continually pestered local farmers for milk to supplement their meagre rations. The petrol shortage was also apparent in the increasing German demands for horses, and in the appearance on the roads of gas-driven lorries. The French here had seen horses harnessed to German cars and lorries, while on D-Day they had been surprised to see wounded

Germans strapped on to bicycles. There were also rumours of gas-driven tanks, but no one to whom I spoke had actually seen one. The Germans were indefatigable in their demands for copper and tyres as well as horses. They even requisitioned butter for the manufacture of engine oil. German morale inevitably suffered as a result of the deteriorating conditions in the army. To the French people of this locality the German soldiers seemed tired, badly fed, homesick and lonely. They had waited a long time for the invasion and were worn out by the state of tension which had lasted since 1941.

French opinion concerning White Russian volunteers in the neighbourhood was not flattering. These Russians did not object either to working for the Germans or to serving in the German army. The Red Russians, however, were different; these men, taken prisoner and conscripted for labour in France, refused to work. They were systematically starved and the story was told of a Frenchman who offered some of these Russians a loaf of bread and was nearly injured in the mad scramble which ensued.

One serious-minded school master said that in 1940, after the fall of France, the people of the country districts were seized with panic at the thought of their country being occupied by a race of butchers and sadists. Some of the more timorous were prepared to live behind bolted doors and never appear in the streets. The reality proved to be far less grim, in appearance at least. The German soldier in France was quite different from some of his compatriots in Poland. The French appeared to have been almost agreeably surprised, experiencing a certain feeling of relief on observing the 'correct' behaviour of the occupying troops. Atrocities did occur whenever the security of the Reich was threatened; for instance, almost a whole community attended the funeral of two RAF pilots, with painful consequences. But the people of the country districts declared that, apart from wholesale requisitioning of meat, grain, vegetables and dairy produce, they were reasonably free from trouble. Towards the end serious attempts to win the friendship of the French had been made by the Germans but without much success.

The mass of the people here were undeniably friendly to Allied soldiers, but there were one or two isolated cases of individuals who appeared to be indifferent, and others who found the effort to be friendly too much for them. Among the latter were people, notably men, who had suffered as a result of RAF raids. The attitude of women towards our raids was noticeably different. Women who had lost home and relatives in raids were everywhere more courageous, more forgiving, and more broadminded than men. Monsieur le Curé quoted the case of a woman at Le Breuil whose husband was killed by an American bomb. She was among the first to welcome the Americans and give them wine. When the *curé* asked her if she bore any grudge she answered that it was not their fault. Her husband had been killed of military necessity by men who had done their duty. Her final remark was a sentence I had already heard in Normandy:

'On ne fait pas d'omelette sans casser des œufs.'

The *curé* was firmly convinced that this woman's attitude was typical of France as a whole. He did not think that our bombing policy would affect the post-war friendship of our two countries.

5

PIGEONS AND PARACHUTES

Journeys outside the camp were a pleasant change when they involved mixing with the village people and listening to their conversations. Other missions, however, produced more sweat than sense: nights were the worst, being the usual time for sudden arousals and calls to arms. There was an occasion when, after midnight, repeated bursts of rifle fire were heard coming from a neighbouring house. Having hardly recovered from the idea of stray bullets said to come from retreating Germans after D-Day, I set out for the village with the support of armed protection. With silent tread and extreme caution we approached the house and made our way through the back door, which had been left open, where instead of the expected enemy sniper we found a drunken American soldier. We were greeted with what appeared to be relief by the owner of the house, a woman, the mother of twelve children, whose husband was away in Germany on forced labour. White-faced and weeping she explained that the man had forced his way into the house and tried to make love to her daughter. When she refused him he went berserk and fired his gun. Luckily no one was hurt.

Then there was the saga of the pigeons. One of our drivers, who had kept pigeons for twenty years, reported having noticed what he described as a regular service of carrier pigeons back and forth between the Mosles district and the Front. He had seen these birds, of which there were three, on more than seventy different occasions. They flew over Tactical Headquarters at regular times: 11.15 a.m., 12.20 p.m. and 3.45 p.m. The same three birds were used every time; they had been trained to fly in two directions, and were a type of bird used for short distances of up to thirty miles. The driver had seen them drop about two miles to the north of the headquarters, near Mosles.

Such careful observations deserved attention, so when the matter was reported to our own captain and sergeant in charge of Signals, all sorts of military authorities as well as pigeon experts began to be involved, including the Operations staff at Tac HQ, the Colonel in charge of Intelligence (British Army), HQ First US Army, Counter-Intelligence Section attached to G2 Branch at V Corps US Army HQ, and 83 Group RAF.

On 22 July it was verified that pigeons were to be seen flying across the camp at the times and in the direction stated by the driver. As a result I was sent for by the major in charge of G (Ops) who suggested our taking compass bearings on the pigeons at the moment of dropping. So, armed with a compass, the driver and I set out on foot in time to catch the 11.15 a.m. pigeon. After having covered six miles across rough country without success, and making enquiries at different US camps, we returned, hot and weary, to our own headquarters. I still have vivid memories of the sweat pouring down my chest and back, and of knees being stung by nettles and spiked by stubble as we crawled across fields and stumbled through hedges in our mad chase after those vindictive birds, which must surely have been enemy inspired.

The next morning, to change the procedure, I lay in wait for the pigeons in a large open field about one mile to the north of the camp, along their line of flight, but they did not make an appearance. In the afternoon the signals sergeant became personally involved when he and I went out in a 15 cwt truck in search of possible users of pigeons. There was no trace of pigeons at the farms on our route and none of the US Army camps visited by us were using them. On 24 July I continued my vigil for an hour in the same large field, then brought the driver to the spot, but no pigeons appeared. What did appear, however, was a lengthy and detailed report.

I was beginning to learn that, in the field of military security, to be a good listener meant being a selective listener, though our driver's story did have more substance than some of the many rumours to which army Intelligence fell victim. But not all chases turned out to be of the wild goose variety. While on my pigeon hunt I was told by the officer in charge of Counter-Intelligence at V Corps US Army that the Czech Todt worker handed over to them by us on 29 June had been classified as highly suspect and passed on to the Master Interrogation Centre.

Another grotesque incident arose from rumours among the civilian population concerning the presence of parachutists in the neighbourhood. To live in our Normandy village during those weeks of world turmoil leading up to and immediately following the painful and protracted struggle for Caen, with the noises of battle rumbling and exploding just beyond the skyline, was to live in an atmosphere wild with rumour and alarm. In comparison life within the camp perimeter was calm. Visits to units in forward positions where men crouched in foxholes under the hail and rattle of machine-gun fire, or were alerted by the whine of approaching shells, made me appreciate my return to the relative tranquillity of Tac HQ.

On one such excursion through the Forest of Balleroy, where fierce fighting had torn the branches off the trees, leaving only ghostly rows of broken stumps, a shell burst uncomfortably close. It toppled me from my motorbike, the blast causing injury to an already damaged eardrum. The damage to the motorbike, undetected at the time, was later to be the cause of trouble.

Village rumours had small beginnings but soon became inflated out of all recognition. The harmless parachute, entangled in a tree, became a parachutist, and from there it was multiplied into the plural. By the time it reached me the story, having been passed from mouth to mouth, had swollen into a wholesale airborne invasion. The remarkable phenomenon was the number of people who claimed to have seen the parachutists. To those of us who were responsible for the security of the headquarters and the physical safety of its Chief, all rumours, true or false, and all personal accounts of parachutists, pigeons, traitors, collaborators, and bursts of gunfire in the night, had to be investigated, regardless of the distances and terrain to be covered, the weather and the lateness of the hour. No time for meals or sleep was sacred when security was threatened, for this was war, nor was there any private property into which we dared not trespass if in search of some malign body. Stately châteaux, humble homes and garden sheds, stables and outhouses, factories and workshops, barns and granaries, churches, convents and monasteries were all equally assailable when the hunt was on, though we rarely entered in the guise or the manner of aggressors and nor were we treated as such. During this time I was alone in the performance of security responsibilities.

Linked with the parachutists rumour was the story of an American reported to have been killed in the Forest of Cerisy by escaped German prisoners supposedly roaming near newly pitched tents. The US soldier had been found near a traffic circle with a knife in his back. American officers added their weight to the general talk by saying that German parachutists had been dropped into the forest during the night. This meant that two separate or two conflicting accounts needed to be verified.

These events involved me in an expedition even more circuitous and no more conclusive than the pigeon expedition, except that I was able to return to camp with a tangible object – one parachute – but no parachutist. After lengthy investigations and more hot, dusty journeys through woods, fields and farms, I eventually tracked down the finder of the parachute. This was Monsieur Perier of Balleroy, a farmhand employed by Monsieur Charles, the Mayor of Montfiquet. He had retrieved it from one of the trees on the farm after a night of heavy bombing. However, the reason for the death of the American remained a mystery.

6

TRAUMA AT FALAISE

Military rites and formalities continued even within the sound of gunfire as, for example, when all camp personnel were paraded for lines inspection. The domestic, social and spiritual life of Tac HQ proceeded as though the war, only a few miles away, were but a temporary interruption of a lifestyle initiated in some cloistered English public school centuries before. It was a situation destined not to last much longer as after the liberation of Caen we were to move nearer to the edge of the cauldron.

I was often required to go alone to a new site to make sure, from a local government officer, or the *gendarmerie*, or sometimes from a prominent citizen or member of Resistance whose name had been given to me, that all was well from the security point of view. Very often names could not be given in the remoter villages into which we penetrated, and I had to reconnoitre for myself. Usually collaborators had already been rounded up or had gone into hiding with the retreating Germans.

Thus we made our way through Normandy, faster now and with shorter stops. In some places we only stayed for a night, and all the labour of striking camp for a sudden departure and pitching tents again on a new site had to be repeated with wearying and increasing frequency. Every move entailed the same routines but with different people. The writing of reports had to be done hurriedly at nights by the shielded light of a torch, or at dawn before the camp was astir.

We invariably camped on the outskirts of villages, in woods or on heathland, never in large towns, much to the disgust and disappointment of many of the men. In fact we had a few cases of acute depression and one suicide attributable, some said, to the gloom of our camp sites, though family worries may have been a more likely cause. There were also two cases of nervous breakdown.

Our arrival in a new village meant that, depending on the length of our stay, I inherited a whole dossier of case histories of collaborators, agents for the German war effort, pro-German sympathisers, soldiers' mistresses and 'doubtful' families. A closer acquaintance with these people, usually through the cooperation of an understanding priest, often revealed a sad history of poverty, temptation, failing courage, and a low morale that was no match for the alluring promises made by the conquerors. For example, the Germans in their propaganda pamphlets had painted such a rosy picture of the payment and privileges enjoyed by workers of the Reich that an impoverished family might volunteer for labour in Germany for the sake of the money. The bulk of hungry French families did not and the hunger was more noticeable, especially among the children, the further we travelled from Normandy and the closer we came to the industrial part of northern France. Our progress towards this area was more rapid now, a sign of the onward push of the Allied Forces. Continued contact with the civilian population brought to my notice the large number of widows and fatherless children in this part of France; their men had either died or disappeared.

It sometimes happened that the mayor, under pressure, had been in the habit of associating with German officers and the *Feldpolizei* during the occupation, on more than official business. Though many mayors raised objections to certain German orders, one whom I met on one of our early moves was conspicuous for having obeyed *all* German regulations, however harsh, without any protest. His conduct was attributed locally more to a love of money than to deliberate collaboration.

The ferocity of the recent battles was becoming more and more manifest. My lonely motorcycle missions to Intelligence sections in both the American and British sectors meant that my journeys were seldom in one direction only, but zigzagged across country from north to south and from east to west. I witnessed some of the dire results of the American 'saturation' bombing. At the approaches to towns and villages further to the west, bomb craters were close to one another with the regularity of holes in a solitaire board. Nothing remained of Aunay-sur-Odon, where bulldozers had made a roundabout by heaping up the shattered remains of the buildings to form a vast central hill topped by a disconnected church steeple leaning tipsily to one side. Among the dusty ruins of St Lô the cinema, sliced open by aerial bombardment, revealed in cross-section the dress circle with rows of plush seats dangling over its stuccoed balcony like bunches of grapes. The most familiar sights, however, were the long processions of refugees of all ages dragging carts laden with their household goods and livestock. There were some farm carts with chicken coops full of birds suspended underneath, others with the farmer's dog walking obediently between the wheels and the horse tethered behind. Other waggons contained newly born calves or other young animals. Sitting perched high on piles of bedding were the old women and the children. The younger women and the few men led the horses or drove the carts.

As the Allied advance quickened, security duties were cut to the speediest interviews with local farmers and military and civil authorities, hurried searches for mines and booby traps before the arrival of the C-in-C, and the gleaning of the latest harvest of rumours and denunciations before the next quick dash in pursuit of front-line forces whose devastations were becoming daily more visible and audible. The scene had changed, now becoming more like my imaginings of the embattled and blighted landscape of the First World War.

On 18 August I called at the Refugee Centre where bombed-out civilians, rescued from the nearby railway tunnel, were living in tents. While the battle of the Falaise gap was in progress on Saturday, Sunday and Monday, the villagers had taken refuge in the tunnel, then returned to find their houses ransacked and pillaged. Even the tiniest hovels had been plundered by the Germans.

The day after the slaughter at Falaise I entered this grim valley while on my usual advance party reconnaissance for the next camp site, and saw the true face of war at its most horrific and repulsive, unrelieved by the camaraderie, the jokes, the diversions and exertions with which men tried to disguise it. In the wreckage of Chambois and Trun little trace of human, animal or plant life remained. At the first of these expunged villages my companions and I noticed a newly dug grave in the garden of what had been a cottage. We knew it was a grave rather than a trench because lying in it on the bare earth was a corpse wrapped in a sheet. There was no coffin. The walls of the cottage, though deeply cracked, were still standing, while doors, windows and roof had been ripped away. Peering into the ruined kitchen we were surprised to see a table set for a meal. The food was untouched, and had only recently been prepared: the house, indeed the whole village, was empty of living people. The signs were that everyone who could had left in a hurry. This eerie yet intimate scene was as puzzling as it was poignant. What could it mean? Had the occupants of the cottage been getting ready for a funeral, their preparations suddenly and savagely interrupted by one of the most massive aerial attacks of the war? And why no coffin? If they had had no time to eat how had they had time to dig a grave?

It was this valley which during the fierce battles of 18 to 20 August became choked with the trapped traffic of German tanks, guns and transport at the mercy of Allied air attack by rocket-firing Typhoons in all their ear-splitting fury. As the gap closed, the escape routes for the German Army had become blocked, not only by rocket and shell fire but also by the wreckage of burning vehicles, by their own exploding ammunition and by the stampeding of terrified horses entangled in their harness, dragging their waggons and gun carriages with them. Ten thousand Germans died in this battle and fifty thousand were taken prisoner.

There was hardly room for my vehicle to pass between the gruesome piles of bodies of men and horses. When our next site beyond Falaise had been chosen I came back through the same dreadful scene, and the following day was on my motorbike again, riding in escort for the main body of Tac HQ. It was here that occurred one of the worst mishaps of my life in Normandy. With the bodies of dead Germans heaped high on each side of the road, my motorbike broke down, and refused to go any further. Meanwhile our convoy moved on, overtook me, passing out of sight to leave me alone. The maintenance of my vehicle was my own responsibility, but this was no routine job and demanded the skill of an expert mechanic and the resources of our Motor Transport (MT) workshop, which unfortunately had disappeared into the distance. The heat was intense, the smell nauseating and I decided to push my motorbike into the shade of a tree which stood up starkly on a hill in front of me in silhouette against the sky. When I reached it I found that it was not a tree at all but the roasted bodies of a German tank crew trapped at waist and knees in the opening of the turret with their blackened arms and charred faces stretched upwards, locked tightly in a frantic effort to escape from their burning tank. It was nightfall when the MT crew, having noticed my absence, eventually made their way back along this road of death to rescue me from my forlorn and grisly vigil. Many of the dead were mere boys, some of them looked no more than fourteen years old. I had taught boys of that age and taken them to Scout camps. There was much to think about during those hours spent in their company. It was not long after arriving in darkness at the new camp site that I was taken ill with dysentry and with what I can only describe as a spiritual sickness involving religious values and anxiety about life and death and human destiny. Why was the reality of war so slow to make its full impact? I don't think it was due to a sluggish imagination. I had seen newsreels of the war, experienced the London Blitz, heard my father talk, sparingly it must be said, about some of the horrors of Mons, Ypres and Passchendaele in the trenches of the First World War, and I had recently taken part in the stirring and disturbing climax of D-Day. Perhaps the truth is that up to that moment I had been enjoying (yes, enjoying!) too much the feeling of being on some unique mission; still intoxicated by the adventure of Overlord and the awareness, encouraged by our politicians and war leaders, of being part of history, and too busy with endless duties to meditate on the larger issues of life and death. The odd church parade was no substitute for such an appraisal. It required five hours of solitary confinement in the company of ten thousand dead men to bring the real message of war home to me.

7

MEMORIES OF MEN OF LETTERS

After a one-day interval to recover from my sickness, my duties were resumed. Each new place repeated the harassments of the old, with variations and additions. There were the usual daily encounters with trespassers, humble petitioners and other disturbers of camp routine. Gunfire during the night led on this occasion not to an inebriated American, but to a trigger-happy Frenchman and a treasure-trove of jettisoned German rifles, hand grenades and a radio. During the day a man from the nearby village called to trade a bottle of Calvados for some tinned foods, and a woman came to us because she had been told that we gave away food. (She must have thought we were Americans.) Some of our would-be trespassers tried to break in with the friendliest intentions.

They came bearing gifts, or seeking gifts in the form of food or souvenirs in exchange for photographs of themselves or their children. Many came to promote the *entente cordiale*, or simply to stand and stare. Others attempted raids upon our swill bins in the search for edible refuse. These were not tramps or vagabonds, but mothers and fathers of families, the lucky beneficiaries of Hitler's glorious Reich.

We began to be aware of the difference in character between the comparatively reserved people of rural Normandy and the ebullient curiosity of the population further east. In Normandy, apart from urgent communications from the civilian community about threats to our welfare, we tended to be left alone to get on with the war. In northeast France the people were all eyes and ears and our work was constantly interrupted by sightseers, informers and denunciators. Some of the information received in this way was useful: we did, for example, catch up with some German soldiers dressed in civilian clothes. A young Frenchman from the Resistance had given us a warning: they had been seen in the neighbourhood of Bellevue, a vast area of wood and heathland. As usual a thorough search was carried out and guards were posted at vulnerable points. Other neighbouring detachments of Second Army had been out on the same quest, for there in 30 Corps POW Cage at Gacé, among ninety-seven Russian, Czech, Polish and Mongolian prisoners I found a number of German soldiers, many in civilian clothes. There could be others. So again we learned not to relax our vigilance though many rumours set us on a false trail. Security was never something that could be left to chance. Our headquarters by its very nature was always in danger and must continuously be regarded as a potential target. What would the stray SS fanatic not give to know who was in those woods or in the secluded corner of that desolate heath? The thought of anything hindering Monty and his plans to win the war for us amounted to nightmare. Fortunately we were so engrossed in doing the job in hand that the force of such worries would only attack us in times of emergency (but then wasn't the whole war an emergency?). In this tense atmosphere, therefore, denunciations of collaborators were still followed up sedulously. There was one particularly classic case of treachery reported to me from both civil and military authorities, the Main HQ 21st Army Group and the FFI. It was alleged that a Frenchman living at St Marc d'Ouilly had collaborated with the Germans during the occupation, traded with them and denounced his compatriots to them. It was reported that he had been seen wearing German uniform and was at that moment wearing British battledress as well as the brassard of the FFI (Free French Forces). Eighteen months earlier he had been to Caen and returned with 25,000 francs. I interviewed two witnesses in Pont d'Ouilly who signed a statement that this man had collaborated with the Germans. This sad story of human frailty is recalled only as a reflection on the mood of unrelenting vengeance against traitors on the part of the French at that time, their refusal to forget betrayal and their insistence that justice be done.

Moments of relaxation became so rare that they have tended to linger in the memory. It was among the citizens of Avernes-sous-Exmes that I experienced one of my strangest and most interesting encounters on the French domestic front. Being responsible for the security of Tactical Headquarters I was in the enviable position of legitimately combining business with pleasure, being duty bound to become as knowledgeable as possible about the political climate of the various rural and urban areas through which military strategy and the fortunes of war obliged the C-in-C to move, as well as enjoying the delightful social contacts inseparable from the serious side of duty. On 27 August 1944 on what must have been a whole afternoon of leisure, I was invited along with Walter Heywood, a draughtsman in G (Ops), to tea with three remarkable and distinguished old ladies. They could be described as either eccentric or liberated, according to taste. The dominant one of the three called herself Madame Bazalgette though she let it be known that she was really Mademoiselle Perrin. She did most of the talking, in a precise, informative, almost pedantic manner, a small, compact, grey-haired lady with old-world courtesy, yet emancipated and progressive in outlook. The others were Madame Kosnick-Kloss and Madame Baksunine, both Russian.

Madame Kosnick-Kloss was more forward-looking and modern in her vision of the world than the nostalgic, hero-worshipping Madame Bazalgette. She was a large, expansive (in every meaning of that word) warm-voiced lady, passionate about art, with the kind of flowing, flamboyant dress associated with Pre-Raphaelite models. Madame Baksunine was quiet and retiring, but charming and hospitable in a gentle way. We were back with the Edwardians, and how happy we both were to be there and to enjoy a moment of respite from bloody war.

Madame Bazalgette had lived as a recluse since the death

of Léon Bazalgette sixteen years earlier. She showed us round the house, kept as a shrine to his memory, in which they had lived together 'defying convention', to use her own expression. The house stood in a solitary, shady, overgrown corner of luxuriant country where the deep silence was disturbed only by the sound of a waterfall in the garden. It was strangely restful to discover this green oasis away from the dust and heat of the sun-baked war-ravaged roads and so near to the ghoulish inferno of the Falaise valley. Passing through the untidy living room we climbed the dark, narrow staircase to the rooms where Bazalgette's memory was treasured, the bedroom and the study overlooking the tranquil garden, alive with the rustle of vegetation and the murmur of running water. A large portrait of the great man faced us as we entered his study, and on the mantelpiece were faded photographs of other famous writers: Emerson, Carlyle, Verhaeren and, in the place of honour, Walt Whitman. Madame Bazalgette had met all these well-known literary figures; she knew Romain Rolland and Georges Duhamel and was at the wedding of Wellington Ku. We were fascinated by her wealth of anecdotes about these men of letters, and her memories of literary gatherings and brilliant soirées at the turn of the last century were not unlike those of Proust. Her one ambition in life had been to be near Bazalgette and to travel the world with him. She would have liked to accompany him when he was invited to dinner by Theodore Roosevelt at the White House but I fancy that this dream was not realised.

Bazalgette was a 'freethinker' and both he and Mademoiselle Perrin were persecuted and ostracized by their families and certain sections of society for their repudiation of organised religion. But they were both deeply religious, if not in the traditional sense; theirs was a humanistic, naturalistic religion in which love of life and faith in humanity featured prominently. Through the progress of modern science and the scientific outlook the happiness and prosperity of the human race were assured. Bazalgette's mature work had been produced before the First World War.

His profession of faith, expounded in the book *L'Esprit Nouveau*, was published in 1898. So here we were in 1944 in the middle of a cataclysmic war, the convulsions of which could be seen and smelt only a mile away, taken gently by the hand and led back into the hopeful company of Claude Monet, Sisley, Pissarro and Renoir and into the Victorian drawing rooms of John Ruskin and Thomas Carlyle. Madam Bazalgette appeared never to have lost the optimistic view of the world which her hero had shared with other nineteenth-century philosophers. According to him the radiant colours of Monet's paintings and the robust earthiness of Zola's characters were expressions of the new spirit – *L'Esprit Nouveau*. The contrast between our recent experience of twentieth-century horror and this escapist glimpse into a long-vanished leisurely world populated by scholars, artists and their idealistic women friends could not have been more extreme.

Walter, who was an artist in civilian life, was interested in what Madame Kosnick-Kloss had to say. She was more concerned with the future than the past. She called herself a 'constructive painter' and was engaged on a project to erect a monument in mosaics to the memory of Bazalgette. Madame Baksunine, a Russian author, spoke of her latest book, which was to be published in France. All three ladies were enthusiastic in their invitation to us to visit the international centre for artists which, in fulfilment of Bazalgette's vision, was to be established in this village after the war. The dear ladies were all elderly and I wonder if their dream ever became reality, as the name of Bazalgette has not appeared in any headlines in the last forty years.

The forward progress of Tac HQ was temporarily blocked by the chaos at Falaise, so Walter and I took time off to pay a second visit to Madame Bazalgette. On this occasion she related more of her literary memories. She said she wanted to classify Bazalgette's library, which should belong to the world. She mentioned a pamphlet which she was intent upon my reading and asked me to wait while she fetched it.

Five minutes later she came back with the paper and a copy of Bazalgette's book. *L'Esprit Nouveau* (*dans la vie artistique, sociale et religieuse*). Her eyes were moist with tears of emotion as she kissed the book twice before giving it to me. She also gave me a piece of shrapnel as a souvenir. I could see that it had cost her an effort to part with the book and I hesitated to take it, but she said that soon she would die and she knew that the book was in good hands because Léon Bazalgette belonged to youth and to the future. She gave me her blessing and kissed me before I left. Madame Kosnick-Kloss and Madame Baksunine also kissed us goodbye and vowed to be our friends for life.

After our civilised tea-party it was a rude shock to come back to the realities of army life, particularly as many of the men had gone down with dysentery. Flies had invaded our camp, bringing infection from the massed corpses in the sweltering Falaise pocket. Movement of the headquarters was further delayed at this point, both by the prevailing sickness and by the continued congestion of traffic in the valley. This brief respite was grasped as an opportunity for the C-in-C to have his portrait painted. For this purpose I had to accompany Captain Henderson, one of Monty's ADCs, to borrow an easel from the village schoolmistress for James Gunn.

Our stay here was not long enough for me to do more than call at the headquarters of the FFI in Gisors to check up on the Duke Pozzo di Borgo, a Corsican of French nationality. His wife was American and patriotic. The Maquis leaders advised the utmost caution in dealing with the duke as he was vice-president of the *Croix de Feu* (a right-wing nationalistic organisation) and a prominent member of the *Cagoulards* (the *Cagoule* was a clandestine French Fascist group in the inter-war years). However, on further enquiry it was revealed that he had never been known to denounce any patriots, while on one occasion he had sheltered a British airman from the Germans for a day.

Then we were on the move with a vengeance. I continued to make the double journey of going with the reconnaissance party and returning to check the security of the move of the main party. No sooner had everybody settled into their new surroundings than I was off again with the advance party to another scene. I left camp at 7 p.m. and after crossing the Seine at Vernon, reached the new camp just before dark. There were brief visits to neighbouring villages and meetings with the inhabitants of Vesly, Noyers and Dangu. Owing to the mileage covered by Tac HQ during the last few days, the speed of subsequent moves and my necessarily hectic life-style, it was decided by G (Ops) that I should leave once and for all with the 'recce' party, there not being time for so many return journeys to look after the main body which was now almost permanently on the move.

We were now entering a region where overt enthusiasm for the Allied effort and resistance to the enemy were more apparent. We were all aware of the change in the emotional climate and were overwhelmed by it. Were these people further east right in their criticism of the Normans for the coolness of their reaction to the liberators? To the English soldiery the Normans may have appeared phlegmatic and reserved, but is that not precisely how the English appear to the majority of French people? Many of us made lasting friendships among the people of Normandy and they have tended not to forget us, as witness the annual ceremonies commemorating D-Day.

On 1 September 1944 Monty was promoted to Field Marshal.

Increasingly now we were coming across people who had taken considerable personal risks to help the Allies. After our crossing of the Seine a party of four American airmen came into the camp with the four Frenchmen who had sheltered them ever since they baled out sixty-seven days earlier. The Americans were given transport back to England; the Frenchmen all wanted to join up. I was then introduced to a middle-aged lady who had given refuge to as many as twenty airmen over a period of seven months.

On our arrival at dusk at another new location a group of FFI youths informed us of the presence of some German soldiers with a machine gun in the wood four hundred yards away. I reported this to Lieutenant Applebee of the Defence Company and patrols were sent out. The danger was real: one of these patriots had been killed while clearing the woods of Germans. The leader of the FFI for this district called at our headquarters to ask if we could be represented in the guard of honour at the funeral and local people were full of gratitude when we sent four men from our Defence Company. It is conceivable that they would have been even more deeply affected had they known that those men represented Field Marshal Montgomery.

Because of the greater demonstrativeness of the population, especially the townsfolk, as we sped through northern France towards the Belgian border, the heavy hand of security did put a damper on the friendliness extended to us, though there were no serious or lasting effects. Stricter controls had to be imposed upon the movement of unauthorised persons and upon the conduct of our troops whenever we settled into a place. However exciting their mission, civilians were not encouraged by our men to enter the camp; notices giving details of our moves were no longer pinned on the notice-board.

On 5 September at 9 a.m. I left with the advance party for our new location at Houtaing in Belgium. A warm welcome awaited us wherever we went in this country, and it started on the first night with an invitation to dinner from the family of Monsieur Leclercq, *Receveur Général* (Treasurer) of Leuze.

8

WELCOME TO BELGIUM

The reception given to our convoy as it passed through northern France, especially in the industrial towns (the first we had seen) of Arras and Douai, where excited crowds lined the streets waving and cheering, was a noisy contrast to the reticent, stunned reaction of the Normans at the time of our surprise landing on their battered beaches. Belgium was even more demonstrative. As our odd collection of eccentric-looking vehicles bumped over the cobbled streets into Tournai, women and children poured out of the houses on to the dusty strips which bordered the road and showered kisses and gifts upon us. It is important to specify women in this instance as many men of military age had been transported to do compulsory labour in Germany. It was September and harvest time, so as we left the town and entered the country we were presented with the many colourful flowers and fruits of the earth: chrysanthemums, dahlias, roses, gladioli, fuchsias and large mauve Michaelmas daisies, luscious pears, plums, greengages, apples and tomatoes. Men travelling in lorries or tanks were more fortunate than I on my motorbike as I required both hands to steer it and had no means of catching the ripe plums and tomatoes which bounced messily off the petrol tank when thrown in my direction.

Compensation was to come when, in the course of security duties at our first Belgian location, I visited the Château de la Berlière occupied by a colony of bereaved and disadvantaged children (*enfants nécessiteux*). Teachers in Belgium proved to be a frequent and reliable source of information in the cause of resistance. I was treated like visiting royalty at this large all-age school, with children forming a guard of honour in the playground as I made my way, firstly to the head teacher's room, then into the hall for school dinner. Before sitting down to what consisted largely of potato soup followed by more potatoes, I was treated to a rendering by the whole school of 'It's a long way to Tipperary'. A speech was of course obligatory; after dinner and a reprise of 'Tipperary', I was dismayed on going out into the playground to discover that my motorbike was nowhere to be seen. I went back into the school, extremely worried, and reported its disappearance to the Head. I was surprised at the apparent casualness of his response to my distress. He simply took me by the arm and escorted me back to the playground where we were followed by a great crowd of children looking like conspirators. They took me to a corner of the playground where I was confronted by my motorbike completely transformed. It had been cunningly and artistically decorated with red, white, and blue flowers – every inch of the metal was covered in flowers. While I was busy at dinner, expert fingers had been at work. They insisted that I drive back to camp without removing a single flower. There was another triumphal guard of honour, joined by people in the street, another chorus of 'Tipperary' by delighted children, and a colourful, if embarrassed, drive back to camp where my friends greeted me with disbelief and much amusement. Needless to say I had to find time to make a return visit to the school.

A Belgian Hero

There were other visits to be made and tasks to be undertaken, both inside and outside the camp area, the boundaries of which became ever harder to define and maintain as crowds of excited Belgians swarmed across the perimeter. They threatened to invade even the most secret of our caravans as well as our living quarters, making the work of security and the guards almost impossible. None of the 'invaders' arrived empty-handed; they came bearing gifts, autumn fruits, the produce of their gardens and farms, always accompanied by kisses, hugs and effusive outbursts of patriotic fervour. Their admiration for our war effort knew no bounds. There were urgent demands from those young men who remained to be linked to it in practical ways; many wanted to join up there and then. It was my immediate and unpopular duty to turn these enthusiastic visitors away. They left reluctantly, only to stand in groups gossiping by the camp entrance, gazing at the sentries.

One woman, however, was not turned away. She was Madame Duquesne, who asked if an officer from our headquarters could visit a patriot who had a remarkable record of courage and endurance during the occupation, and was now lying bed-ridden with a broken back, the direct result of his resistance activities.

Fernand Gennotte had been a first-year medical student at the University of Louvain when in March 1943 he was ordered to report for work for the Germans. He refused and in May of that year during a police raid in Tournai he was arrested and sent to a Nazi prison in the Boulevard Léopold. From there he was condemned to forced labour in a foundry near Dortmund, and though under extreme pressure to do so, he never gave away the names of his compatriots. After two unsuccessful attempts to escape he finally succeeded, made his way back to Belgium and joined the *Armée Belge des Partisans* (PA). During this time he took part in a number of dangerous expeditions, transporting arms and ammunition, sheltering Allied airmen, sabotaging railway lines and penetrating German positions dressed as a German soldier.

On the night of 6 June 1944, following a coded message from the BBC, the partisans' group of the Péruwelz sector under the command of Raymond Bachy (code name 'Roland') their *chef de Résistance*, were out in a field waiting for the dropping by parachute of arms destined for the Resistance. The weather was stormy, with strong winds and driving rain. Some of the parachutes became entangled in the trees and 'Nandy' (Fernand) climbed a tall, slender poplar in an attempt to dislodge a container which, with its parachute, had wrapped itself around the topmost branches. With the added weight of the man and the force of the gale a branch snapped and Fernand fell to the ground followed by the heavy ammunition box, which crashed on to his back as he lay there and severed his spine. The enemy were concealed only a few hundred metres away and there was a sudden burst of gunfire in which two of the partisans were wounded. Under cover of darkness Nandy's comrades managed with the aid of a ladder used as a stretcher to transport him to shelter where, in great pain, he was given first aid. A few days later he was taken secretly by ambulance to the Institute of St Raphael in Louvain University where he was hidden in the maternity wing and operated on – he was paralysed from the waist down.

At the time of our arrival in this remote village he was at his parent's home, hoping for a glimpse of the 'liberators' for whose common cause Belgians and their allies had struggled.

Madame Duquesne finished her story and expressed the hope that someone 'from England, a soldier, perhaps an officer, perhaps even Field Marshal Montgomery himself' might come to see their hero. The Chief was not in the camp, but Lieutenant Colonel Kirke agreed to visit the young man at 6 o'clock that evening. However, at the appointed time I received a message from Colonel Kirke that at the last moment pressure of work prevented him from coming with me to see the wounded patriot. He was genuinely sorry not to be able to make this small sympathetic gesture. Fernand therefore had to be content with my visit. It meant going on the motorbike. The journey through the woods to the isolated hamlet of Moustier where he lived was rough and muddy and Madame Duquesne had warned me that I might meet some German stragglers hiding in the undergrowth.

The family were grouped round Fernand's bed when I

arrived and we enjoyed an evening of lively, friendly conversation. He asked for his bed to be moved to the window when I left so that he could wave goodbye. His mother wrapped up some tarts for me to take away, and his younger sister Hélène placed a bunch of asters on my bike. It was now dark and I was guided through the wood by the young brother, Jean-Marie, on my pillion to the farm of Monsieur and Madame Duquesne where I had supper.

It was while I was in Belgium, and later in Holland, that I was able to gain a fuller picture of what the war meant to the ordinary people – some of them by no means ordinary – of occupied Europe. Apart from the long siege of Caen when Tac HQ was at a standstill on the lonely farm of François Hamel in Blay, our passage through Normandy was so swift that with the exception of my encounter with H28 and the fraternity in Bayeux there had been little time to meet Resistance groups, who surfaced more noticeably in the larger centres of population usually avoided by General Montgomery. On approaching Brussels and later Eindhoven, however, I was to come into closer contact with what being in the Resistance really meant. No words of mine, in this personal account of wartime experiences, can do justice to the heroism which such membership implied. Through Fernand I came nearer to an understanding of these realities than I had been before, and talking with Madame Duquesne and her large family gathered round the supper table on that highly emotional night, I was privileged to share their joy at a newly-won liberation, but without having suffered the long drawn-out agony of the preceding struggle. All patriots had been at risk, whether as active members of the Resistance or as sympathisers with them.

There were stories of heroes who died rather than betray their comrades, of torture as the price of silence, of steadfastness before the firing squad, of faint voices crying out over crackling radio transmitters: 'They've got me. Warn the others.' I listened to accounts of incredible dangers being faced by men, women and children: of ambush at street corners, of parachutes that failed to open, of madness and suicide, of overwhelming fear and superhuman bravery; of the widespread disappearances of loved ones and the anxious waiting for news that never came.

Walthère Dewe, born in Liège in 1880, was one of the greatest Belgian leaders of the Resistance. He was the founder of subversive communications networks for the Allies in two world wars. It was he who gave advance warning to the British, Belgian and French governments of the imminent invasion by Germany of the Low Countries in 1940. After the Belgian capitulation in the same year Dewe adopted the life of an outlaw, continuously on the move, taking shelter where he could and in such circumstances developed a nationwide organisation of underground information. He was able to recruit over fifteen hundred agents to this work, which penetrated into France, Holland and even Germany. The network established permanent radio contact with Great Britain, and the resistance continued; thanks to parachutists, cross-country couriers and radio transmissions.

The London-based Belgian government consulted Dewe on all major decisions concerning the liberation of their occupied country. His incessant activity for the cause of resistance was bound to lead to great vigilance on the part of the occupying power. Then tragedy overtook him. In January 1943 his wife, who had collaborated closely with him throughout two world wars and was so often interrogated by the enemy about his manoeuvres, collapsed and died of a heart attack. His two daughters were arrested and taken to Ravensbrück concentration camp, from which one of them did not return. Walthère Dewe, on his way to warn a seventy-nine-year-old fellow conspirator of a grave danger which threatened her, was waylaid by the Gestapo and beaten to death at a street corner as he tried to escape.

Many others perished in prisons and concentration camps. Dominique Potier, born in 1903, used his experience as a pilot in the service of the Resistance. Having made his way via France, Spain and Portugal to London in 1942 he applied for service with the RAF but was turned down because of his age. Nevertheless he was authorised to plan an escape route through Spain for airmen shot down over enemy territory. Returning by parachute to the continent he was then able to serve the air forces indirectly. At Rheims he was betrayed by an informer, arrested and tortured. In spite of interminable cross-questioning he remained silent. As one agony was heaped on another by his torturers, including the excruciating removal of an eye, he felt that he was reaching the limits of his endurance. Not wanting to endanger his comrades in a moment of weakness, he took advantage of a lapse in vigilance on the part of his guards and leapt to his death from an upstairs window.

Charley Claser, born in 1901, was another active fighter against the army of occupation. He had been a regular soldier and like Dewe he travelled across country under a variety of assumed names. He gathered round him a large number of patriots and founded *La Légion Belge*. At the beginning of 1941 this movement joined with another created by Colonel Robert Lentz. This new formation was later called the *Armée de Belgique* and then *Armé Secrète*. Its main object was resistance against the occupying forces by means of sabotage and the development of a military strength which would strike at the critical moment dictated by Allied command. It also had a positive aim, namely to secure law and order and the maintenance of national institutions after the departure of the Germans. In this endeavour the *Armée Secrète* obeyed a strict code of traditional military discipline. In 1942, travelling through France and Spain where for a while he was interned, Claser managed to get away to England. Landing there on 22 July he made contact with the British SOE (Special Operations Executive) and armed with a plan for future operations, returned to Belgium.

Meanwhile during Claser's absence Colonel Lentz and the other leaders of the *Légion Belge* (as it had been called formerly) had been arrested. To add to his misfortunes Claser lost contact with England when the promised radio operator failed to arrive. He decided to return across the Channel but on his way through France was arrested by the enemy. Under interrogation he maintained the most rigorous silence, for which he suffered hideous tortures.

He was a giant of a man, of powerful physique, but in the concentration camps of Gross-Strehlitz and Gross-Rozen during the bitter winter of 1944 (the terrible winter of the Ardennes offensive) he was reduced to a skeleton. Throughout his captivity he was noted for his exemplary dignity under many trials and humiliations and considered a saint by the other prisoners. He was stripped of his clothes and transported across the camp to the huge ovens where he was burned. His ashes were scattered to the winds.

The role of women in the Resistance was of paramount importance, not least in the moral support they gave, while still carrying on with their everyday work. They were also given quite specific assignments as couriers transporting false papers, ration cards, passports, clandestine journals, messages and even arms. They acted as guides to escort prisoners to freedom. There were many who remained anonymous and gave sanctuary in their homes to Jews, to Allied airmen, to patriots under threat and to desperate members of the Resistance until such time as the escape route became clear. They harboured radio transmitters and the senders of messages. For these crimes many of them paid with their lives after deportation to concentration camps.

Marguerite Bervoets, a distinguished student of philosophy and the arts, taught French literature at the École Normale in Tournai. After the terrible bombing of that town in May 1940 and the invasion of Belgium by German armed forces, she joined *La Légion Belge*.

Her principal activities in the Resistance Movement were gathering information and assisting Allied parachutists to escape across the Belgian border to France and eventually to England, and, most dangerous of all, providing the use of her house as an arsenal. In August 1943, while on a mission to take photographs of an airfield at Chièvres, she was arrested, imprisoned, and sentenced to death. One year later, on 7 August 1944 (one month after D-Day and a few weeks before the liberation of Belgium), she was beheaded with an axe at Wolfenbüttel prison.

Sometimes whole families sacrificed themselves for the cause of resistance. Such was the case of the Lambrechts family from Limbourg. Tony Lambrechts was Head of Resistance and Commander of the *Armée Secrète* in Limbourg, and in constant touch with the Belgian Government in London. After well-planned efforts to rescue other members of the Resistance who were in prison, the family was betrayed. Three of Tony's brothers (one of them a priest) and their father were shot. Their sister was deported to a concentration camp. Tony survived to lead his army in battle at the liberation of Limbourg and was awarded the DSO.

Children were also actively involved in the struggle. Fifteen-year-old Jacques Jansen made a habit of climbing the stairs of the belfry in Liège, and using this lofty perch as his observation post would give regular reports to the Resistance about the movements of the German garrison stationed below. This information eventually led to the success of American forces in September 1944 in their attack on enemy tanks and to the subsequent liberation of the town. Carried away by his enthusiasm, the boy hurried to the top of the bell tower, which overlooked the German barracks, still occupied by four hundred encircled SS fanatics. There he unfurled the Belgian flag for all to see. Inevitably he was seen by the enemy and, still waving his flag, became a target for small arms fire. He died two days later.

Thinking of these stories, taken at random from the wider population of unknown heroes, makes one think how sad it is that such gifts of brain and heart, physical stamina, courage and humour, not to mention professional skills indispensable for the peaceful business and happiness of the human race, should have to be sacrificed on the altar of war. Sadder still to contemplate that, in spite of these sacrifices, tyrants and tortures have not been banished from our world.

LIBERATION FEVER IN BRUSSELS

Uprooted from one place to another in such rapid sequence and bombarded with so many contrasting emotions, from the wild excitement of a whole town to the mute anguish of individuals, I was in danger of becoming inoculated against any genuine feeling at all. From the desolation of Falaise to the delirium of Brussels was only a matter of days. I was also becoming too busy.

So, with my mind still obsessed by images of the youthful, stricken Fernand, I was off again with the advance party to a new location where, in a different set of circumstances, my first job was still to look after the security of Tac by anticipating all the possible dangers confronting it. I therefore contacted the Chief of the *Brigade Blanche*, who had been most thorough in removing likely obstacles to our advance and assured me that since the arrest and imprisonment of two families of collaborators all was now quiet in the village. A German prisoner was also brought to me and, after questioning, I handed him over to the *Brigade Blanche* for transport to the nearest POW camp.

The irrepressible Belgians were still trying to make their way into our new settlement with mixed motives of generosity and curiosity. Gifts were continually being handed to the sentries for distribution to officers and other ranks. Our sign *Défense d'entrer* had no effect. I also asked the priest to persuade the people to stay away and leave us in peace to get on with the war (strange contradiction), but as soon as one crowd of civilians was turned away others arrived. We were now getting sightseers from other villages and even from Brussels. This was a remarkable contrast to the tranquil farm of Monsieur Hamel in Normandy where the Chief came and went without fuss. Here at Houtaing the identity of Field Marshal Montgomery was clearly detected in this quiet village from the day of his arrival, with obvious problems for security. In order to disperse the ever-increasing crowd of sightseers and souvenir hunters I finally had to address them through a megaphone. An appeal to their patiotism seemed to work the miracle and they disappeared. We were never disturbed here again, though similar greetings awaited us in other parts of Belgium, Holland and, strangest of all, in Hamburg in the Reich itself.

Our new camp was in the grounds of the château of the Prince de Mérode, from whom I obtained the required list of people residing and working on the estate. The château had been used as billets by the German Luftwaffe. This camp was also besieged by villagers, none of whom came empty-handed. We were once more overwhelmed with apples, pears, plums, tomatoes and flowers, and children collected wood for our cookhouse fire. I asked the people to leave, and the Military Police received instructions to place notices in Flemish stating that entry to the camp was forbidden. Two officers of the *Brigade Blanche* visited us and offered to supply patrols for our protection. Though we held ourselves responsible for our own protection we left them free to decide whether they would patrol or not. They wanted a password to avoid clashes with our Defence Company during the night. I had already made contact with Monsieur Mangin, Chief of Police and of the *Brigade Blanche* at Cortenberg, and after consultation with the Defence Company and the Tank Crew it was decided to cooperate in patrolling the neighbourhood of the camp. I was later able to report to Monsieur Mangin that the men were beginning to recognise the patrols of the *Brigade Blanche* and no password was necessary. Their official designation *police militaire* sufficed. With so much vigilance peace was restored to our tented village after the excitements of the day.

A journey into Brussels on 9 September proved to be one long celebration which reached a frenzied climax on the 10th, the first Sunday of liberation for the capital. At the sight of men in British battledress women would run and kiss us; the men thrust bottles of beer into our hands. Everywhere there was drinking and dancing, in and out of doors. It is doubtful whether there have ever been anywhere so many invitations to dinner, to supper, to breakfast – to bed – as in Brussels during those days of liberation fever. Many marriages were made in haste in the general atmosphere of intoxication, and Tac HQ was not exempt; one of our Cockney lads married a countess and a few others had narrow 'escapes'. One result of the all-night festivities was that I missed the last tram back to the camp (we were as usual in the country), stayed overnight in the town and after catching the first tram in the morning had an hour's walk across muddy fields from the tram-stop. Again it was characteristic of our lonely headquarters that it was never situated near to anything as urban or convenient as a tram- or bus-stop.

The next few days in the heady vicinity of Brussels were divided between the routine chores of camp life and the extended jollifications and relaxations enjoyed with the civilian population. I was still busy investigating denunciations (how the Belgians hated the Germans, but with how much greater venom did they loathe the traitors!), shots fired during the night and going out on patrols shared with the *Brigade Blanche*. I continued coping with petitions addressed to Field Marshal Montgomery, listening to stories of the Resistance and of people to whom the recent weeks had brought tragedy and bereavement, as well as trying to find answers to give to those who came to the camp attempting to exchange their home-grown tomatoes for our tins of margarine. But I was also going to dances, to *soirées musicales* in private houses, drinking tea laced with Cointreau and playing the piano in the village café. My own discipline began to suffer along with that of other servicemen of all ranks. I found myself oversleeping and missing breakfast, as detailed reports still had to be written in spite of the endless exchanges of war experiences between civilians and military, in spite of the invitations, the laughter, the jokes, the tears, the music, the coffee, the grapes and the wine. One of our happiest visits was to a monastery where the monks regaled us with alcohol and wanted to try on our uniforms. There was also shopping to be done for relatives and friends at home, as many of the shops in Brussels were inviting, and bright with wares unseen in wartime London.

Among Monty's goodwill gestures during the liberation in Brussels was attendance at the Embassy Church followed by a visit to patients in the hospital, at both of which places I was required for security duties.

Our brief Brussels honeymoon ended for me when I had to leave with the advance party to reconnoitre the next place on our route through Belgium. It was during this period of hope in the development of the war that a letter from home gave me further uplift, with the news that dim-out had replaced black-out in Britain.

The night before the departure of the reconnaissance party Tac HQ celebrated by giving a dance to which all the inhabitants of Cortenberg came, all except the house-bound and severely disabled. Old and young arrived, all with shopping bags. During the interval, refreshments, consisting of free beer and sandwiches, disappeared into the shopping bags, followed by the disappearance of all our guests and dancing partners.

At the new site the boot was on the other foot when we sampled food left behind by Germans who had retreated in a hurry. We had toasted German bread for tea and German sausage and honey for breakfast. Inspection of our surroundings involved a tour of the village and an interesting visit to a convent of cloistered nuns vowed to silence. Only one of them was permitted to talk to me, and this though an iron grille.

9

HUNGER IN HOLLAND

On Saturday 23 September we watched droves of gliders being towed towards the Front, an incredible sight. Not until later did we hear about the Arnhem gamble. I had hardly recovered from the spectacle of this airborne armada when I was brought gruesomely to earth by another reminder of what the war was all about. At Hechtel, in a clearing in the middle of a fir plantation near where we had pitched our tents, I stumbled upon an execution firing range. There were four wooden stakes and butts riddled with bullet holes and approximately two hundred graves in an adjoining clearing, indicated by posts each bearing a number engraved on a metal tab.

During the night the heavy clouds were lit up spasmodically by flashes of gunfire at the Front. The noise of war grew louder as our advance party, now more regularly on the move, approached the Dutch border. It was near the town of Weert that I had an experience which was the first link in a chain of remarkable coincidences which would ultimately stretch over forty years. One of the Chief's ADCs needed confirmation of the suitability, from the security point of view, of our next camping place in Holland. I was given the name of a Mr Kuipers who lived in the small village of Budel not far from Weert. He had been an active member of the Resistance during the very recent occupation. The C-in-C's caravan needed, as always, cover from the air and security against possible collaborators and saboteurs on the ground. All likely suspects must be cleared from the area before the arrival of our main body. It was early morning, sunny and fresh, and I was looking forward to my first visit to Holland. I crossed the frontier and in Budel saw a boy of about nine playing alone in the quiet, empty street.

'Hello,' he said as I stopped the motorbike.

His response to my own greeting gave me perfect confidence in his understanding and knowledge of English.

'Do you know Mr Kuipers,' I asked 'and where he lives?'

'He's my father. I can take you to him.'

'What's your name?'

'Paul.'

'Well, Paul, get on the back of my bike.'

It was a rough ride, ending along a narrow path raised high like a dyke between two stretches of water. At the end of this tightrope was a single house surrounded by willow trees. The front door opened on to an immaculate black and white tiled Dutch interior. Mr Kuipers was hospitable, friendly and cooperative and offered me a glass of Bols gin. Paul showed the usual boyish signs of excitement and pride in his father's reputation. The name Montgomery was never mentioned. Contact was made later that day with the Dutch police and the village, as far as could be ascertained, was established as 'secure'. To the local people I was simply a British soldier gathering information about a camp site for an army unit. This unremarkable event was to have a sequel long after the end of the war in Europe.

The entry in my diary for 23 September reads: 'I now have a bed in the tent.' This made a welcome change from sleeping on a groundsheet, especially in Holland with the approach of autumn mists and fogs. I celebrated this new acquisition with a mug of tea, biscuits, corned beef, chocolate and an apple in the tent before going to bed.

Food was an urgent priority among the civilian population. Once when we had supper in a fir plantation by the swimming pool, the Ijzeren Man our next camp site in Eindhoven, we were watched by hungry women and children, but prevented by army regulations from openly sharing our rations with them. On another occasion I asked a Dutch friend where all the people were, as everybody in the town looked so young. She replied:

'Many of the old died long ago.'

One exception was the grandmother of Inge and Hilmar, two young Dutch people who gave a party for us at their beautiful home. They lived with their grandmother during the absence of their parents, the father having left the safety of liberated Eindhoven for a dangerous mission to friends in the Resistance in the still occupied north of Holland, the mother away visiting relations. At the party, for seven Dutch girls, one Dutchman and seven English soldiers, we played parlour games. It was all very seemly and our men were at first subdued, though obviously enjoying these simple, unsophisticated pleasures, in contrast to the rigours and crudities of camp life on the one hand and the recent temptations of Brussels on the other. Tragedy was to strike this family after our departure from Eindhoven (see Epilogue).

It was at this time, with the Allied push into Germany imminent, that security at Tac HQ was intensified and my lonely efforts were supplemented by the addition of an Intelligence section. I was at first independent of these new arrivals, but then it was considered more rational that I should become part of the section, henceforth to be known as the Tac HQ Counter-Intelligence Detachment, CI Detachment for short. We were to be equipped with jeeps in readiness for the assault on Germany, so on Sunday 1 October 1944 I reluctantly parted with my motorcycle and, with mixed feelings, relinquished my role of lone rider.

Soon after this, on 3 October, three of us went on detachment to Nijmegen to make contact with Corps and Divisional sections. We saw the wreckage of many gliders and houses burning. A pall of smoke covered the town and during the heavy shelling of the bridge we sheltered in a cellar, which we shared with another intelligence section, with Dutch refugees turned out of their homes by Germans, and with other Dutch civilians sheltering from the explosions. Sleep was impossible with the continuous shelling of the town and we emerged from our subterranean shelter to a noticeable change of scene. Fortunately for us, though the car parked in our front garden had been completely smashed by a shell, our jeep in the garden next door was undamaged.

Accommodation, especially somewhere to sleep, was a problem in this war-scarred town full of homeless people and army units sharing the available rooms amongst themselves and with displaced civilians. Being an intelligence section on detachment for what must have seemed to front line fighting troops to be both vague and irrelevant in the desperate circumstances, we had some difficulty in securing an official billet for ourselves. The only solution was to find unofficial sleeping quarters, and we were lucky enough to meet a boy who was willing to let us sleep in a loft on straw with other refugees. I still had to write reports and somehow managed to snatch odd moments to do this. Added to the din of shells bursting was the noise of raids by German bombers and the answering heavy fire by our anti-aircraft guns.

Along the roads full of tanks we tried to find 57 Field Security Section but in the confusion, after being jammed in a close-packed, slow-moving convoy, we found 19 Field Security Section instead. After reporting back to Tac, two of us, Gerry Chamberlain and I, drew two days' rations and were on the road again. We were fortunate this time in finding a room in a small café cum hotel, Het Witte Huis, in Grave. We gave the landlady all our army rations and agreed to eat there, using only our own food, and not drawing on the scanty provisions of the Dutch. It was with some surprise then that at dinner with the proprietor's family there was no sign of our corned beef or our 'compo' stew, but we were confronted with some dark brown meat, stringy and very tough. I thought it might be rabbit and with an effort we both struggled through it. I asked what kind of meat it was. One woman quietly murmured:

'Miaow.'

I stared at her.

'You don't mean . . . ?'

Whereupon a young woman flared up:

'It's all very well for you English. You don't know what it means to starve, to have to eat your own pets.'

Gerry looked decidedly green and we rose to leave. Outside the café Gerry walked through the side gate into the small back yard.

'Where are you going?' I asked.

He lifted the lid of a dustbin and peered inside.

'Come and look at this.'

I looked inside and there lay the black and white skin of a cat. Gerry was immediately sick into the dustbin.

Our duties for Tac involved another visit to 19 Field Security Section and one to 45 Section to ascertain if the security picture was clear for the forward movement of the HQ. It was with some relief when the time came for us to return to base, but on the night before our departure there was a party in Het Witte Huis. It seemed that the state of siege was over and liberation assumed its now familiar pattern of universal rejoicing though, in a starving population, with less abandon than in Brussels.

Life in Eindhoven was peaceful and almost normal compared with the racket of Nijmegen. On our first night back Gerry and I enjoyed some relaxation at a film show in town. Bing Crosby playing a priest in *Going My Way* belonged to a different world.

As our stay in Eindhoven was prolonged many friendships blossomed between the British troops and Dutch civilians. In my quest for churches for Monty's regular Sunday services I was taken by my friends Inge and Hilmar to see a Protestant minister, Mr van der Heijden, with the object of using his church for our church parade – he readily agreed to this. Other requests followed and as I was making daily visits to see Inge she became a willing ambassador between me and the van der Heijden family. I was invited to musical evenings at the manse. Elizabeth, one of the daughters, sang; her fiancé Klaas played the violin; her sister Meta the flute; and

I played the piano. The parents were our audience. In the 'interval' we had a small helping of stewed apple. There was very little else to eat.

One day one of the sentries at the camp handed me a letter. It was from Klaas telling me that Elizabeth had been taken seriously ill and her life was in danger due to lack of nourishment. With the letter was some money for me to buy chocolate for her at our canteen as the shops in Eindhoven were empty. The letter was full of apologies for doing what he knew to be illegal and against army rules, and I must on no account tell the family, but he was deeply worried. I took the letter and showed it to the officers' mess cook. He said:

'Come back at six o'clock with your kitbag.'

That evening I made my way with the jeep and a kitbag full of tins of meat, salmon and margarine, bread, biscuits, rice and vegetables. Balanced on the top of this feast was a large bunch of purple grapes.

'We bought these this afternoon in Brussels,' said the cook and jerking his thumb in the direction of the officers' mess, 'they're not going to miss them.'

At the home of Mr van der Heijden I asked if I could go in their kitchen.

'Certainly, but what for?'

In front of the astonished family and the embarrassed-looking Klaas I began to unload the cargo of food on to their kitchen table. There was silence at first then the whole family burst into tears. We had a beautiful evening of music after the first waves of excitement and explanation had died down, but there was not a word about Klaas' letter. Klaas played a Mozart violin sonata, Meta played Beethoven's sonata Op. 27, No. 2 in C sharp minor ('Moonlight'), then Debussy's 'Arabesques' on the flute. Elizabeth sang French songs.

There were emotional goodbyes that night as I left. I had made lasting friends in Holland, at the expense of Monty's cookhouse. During the rest of our stay in Eindhoven many pleasant evenings were spent with the van der Heijden family. We had long discussions about education, literature, politics, religion, pacifism, the Germans and always there was music, in which army friends of mine sometimes joined.

On 12 October Captain Henderson, one of Montgomery's ADCs, sent for me asking if I could borrow from my Dutch friends a cushion and a footstool. He explained that HM King George VI was to visit the headquarters at which there was to be an investiture. A number of officers were to receive decorations from the king. At this ceremony the recipients would have to kneel before His Majesty and the medals and other decorations would be displayed and presented to the king on a cushion before being awarded. For security reasons the king's visit was to be kept secret.

I went to the van der Heijdens and asked if I might borrow a footstool. Without asking any questions they said:

'You can have whatever you like.'

I was taken to the pastor's church where a handsome footstool was offered to me. Back at the house I ventured another request:

'There is something else. Have you a cushion I could borrow?'

'Of course.'

This led to a search all over the house.

'Choose which one you like.'

'I like them all, but they're not for me. I'm afraid they are not suitable.'

There were chintz cushions, woollen cushions, some with large orange flowers, other with Regency stripes.

'We don't want to know what it is for, but can you give us some idea?'

Trying to avoid giving away the secret of the royal visit I talked about churches and cathedrals and things appropriate to solemn gatherings. Elizabeth ran upstairs exclaiming:

'I've got just the thing for you.'

She came down carrying a deep red-wine coloured silk evening dress in one hand and a pair of scissors in the other.

'What are you going to do?'

'Make you a cushion.'

'Oh, no. Not with that.'

I moved forward to stop her but she slashed at the dress with the scissors.

'Now it's no longer a dress, and the cushion will be ready for you tonight.'

When I took the footstool and the beautifully made cushion wrapped in tissue paper to Captain Henderson he was conspicuously impressed.

'This is new. Where did you buy it?'

'I didn't buy it, Sir. It was specially made.'

On Sunday 15 October there was a church parade followed by the investiture at which, inspite of security, the press were present. On the next day the newspapers carried a picture of one of Monty's liaison officers kneeling on Mr van der Heijden's footstool, and the king bearing in his hands Elizabeth van der Heijden's cushion on which rested the various awards for military distinction. The news of the king's visit spread quickly through Eindhoven. I cut the picture out and took it to the van der Heijden family along with a 'certificate' I had made, sealed with sealing wax and bound with a piece of ribbon to which I had somehow managed to give an official appearance. At the house I asked all the family to gather round and ordered Elizabeth to kneel down. Another investiture was about to take place. I read out the citation on the mock certificate, ending with the words:

'I hereby appoint Elizabeth van der Heijden Royal Needlewoman to His Majesty King George VI.'

The family was honoured in an authentic way when Mr van de Heijden gave the address on the radio in a religious broadcast to the Dutch people in thanksgiving for the liberation. I was invited to the house to listen to the broadcast, a moving experience, especially for the family who knew at first hand what starvation and survival meant. The day after Elizabeth's 'investiture' we had another musical party and the picture of the king with the cushion was in a frame on the piano next to the 'certificate'.

On 21 October the C-in-C addressed his own Tactical Headquarters in the back room of a café (an indication of the modest size of this HQ at that time). He said that the war in Europe was conducted from Tac, and thanked us all for our work, emphasising that every man was important and necessary for the success of the operations.

On 22 October came the news of the fall of Aachen and Belgrade. Another message nearer home was a phone call from Captain Coleman, Intelligence Corps, ordering three of us to report to I. Corps Headquarters in Brussels for Intelligence 'work'. We packed our kit and left for Brussels in the jeep. On arriving there we were told that the job was off but we could have forty-eight hours' leave. (I could not help wondering whether this was going to be the pattern from now on, as the security jobs formerly done by one person were now in our reinforced headquarters, shared among six people.) Whatever the reason for the alteration we welcomed the break and intended to make the most of it.

It was over Brussels that I saw flying bombs for the first time and, after the ominous silence when their engines cut out, heard them explode. So this was Hitler's secret weapon? Here too I saw people searching garbage bins for food. Accommodation during this surprise leave in Brussels was no problem as I was able to find lodgings with my old friends of 50 Field Security Section who were billeted in what had been the Gestapo Headquarters. I had not seen my friends since before D-Day when I was taken from them to join Tac HQ. They were not slow to show me some of the horrors which they had inherited, including a room on the top floor which at first glance appeared to be a dentist's surgery, but on closer inspection was seen to be a place reserved for torture, complete with sinister furnishings and instruments. With a shiver I came downstairs to be greeted with a reassuring mug of tea, and bread and jam. My old friends could not have been more kind and hospitable and there was every comfort in that spine-chilling place, but I felt there was something to be said for the austerity of a tent in Monty's country hide-out. The Forces personnel in Main HQ 21 Army Group had come direct to Brussels from England and had not had any contact with the devastation of Normandy or the hunger of Holland. They were later to be confronted with the plight of defeated Germany.

For the time being, however, the three of us who were off duty were not too preoccupied with austerity, as the army in Brussels had gone out of its way to make life as pleasant as possible for troops on leave. I visited other old friends that day and called at the monastery in Avenue de Tervueren, then went on a sight-seeing walk to the Grand' Place, the Manneken Pis and the Royal Palace. In the evening I was invited with other soldiers to dinner at a private house with a family. The next day we loitered along the boulevards watching the people, especially an elaborate procession outside the Church of Sainte Gudule. We had ices topped with fruit (unheard of in Eindhoven) and on our way back to our billets hung on to the side of a crowded tram as there was no room inside. We had our photographs taken, went to a cinema where we saw *Champagne Charlie*, had a both at the public baths (*Bains Modernes*) in Boulevard Anspach and spent the evening at the Sergeants' Club. Here I met an ATS driver to whom I told Elizabeth van der Heijden's story and she gave me all her chocolate ration to give to her.

At the end of forty-eight hours' respite we had a cold, windy journey back to Tac where a welcome pile of letters from home awaited me. Flying bombs were making their presence felt there too and became a new source of anxiety.

From the beginning of the campaign in Europe, when emergency rations and sweets were issued, we had all been given reminders about an army having to march on its stomach, and lectures warning us against giving our sweets away to children, as the 'energy was needed to fight'. Nevertheless it was not a comfortable feeling to be enjoying our adequate army rations among a starving population. All the men who had Dutch friends smuggled food out to them, nobody stopped us, all soldiers broke the rule, from Normandy onwards, where children were concerned, even in Germany.

Soon after my return from Brussels I was away again on detachment in the Dutch town of Mill, where I was billeted with a family. On my first morning with them I got up early and had to wash and shave in the kitchen. The children were there eating their breakfast of dry bread and boiled onion tops.

Returning to Tac on 27 October, I wrote my report. It included an account of the food situation in Brussels where a thriving black market provided food for the rich, and dustbins were searched for barely eatable contents by the poor. In Holland the hunger was universal, among rich and poor alike.

The main preoccupation of the CI Detachment, however, was the security of Tactical Headquarters. Check-ups on residents of Eindhoven had to be made and were more complicated than my earlier exploits in the Normandy villages. They were not the outcome of denunciations, as in the French context, but rather a reflection of the need for tighter security in an urban environment. Here enemy infiltration was more likely to go undetected, especially by so small a headquarters as ours. This was the reason for our frequent forays in quest of information from other neighbouring intelligence units, and why it was necessary for continuous communication with them.

To get back to Tac and its routines was like coming home. I resumed my visits to the van der Heijden family, taking with me supplies of corned beef, M and V (tinned meat and vegetable stew) and chocolate for Elizabeth, then spent the evening listening to music. Just as the thought of Normandy revives the memories of summer heat and dusty roads against the chaotic background of war, so my recollection of Eindhoven is of a mellow autumn sun shining through the yellowing leaves of the avenue leading to the van de Heijden home, and of starry nights on my walks in the black-out back to camp.

It seemed a long way from the crumbling farmhouses and peeling paintwork of Normandy to the scrubbed brick walls, neat casements and tidy hedges of these Dutch villas (though shattered Nijmegen had shown us what scant respect a war could spare for civic pride). All our previous locations had been rural ones, either on the outskirts of small villages, on isolated farmland or in the depths of a wood, where security was largely a matter of careful patrolling. Eindhoven was our only urban camp site. Later, Germany and the gloom of pinewoods were to become for us almost synonymous.

The sense of foreboding compounded by the unknown prospect before us and the approach of winter was reinforced by a visit on 3 November from a Lieutenant Johnson from a neighbouring unit, reporting that three of his men had seen a British soldier dragged out of the nearby canal – his legs had been tied.

Gerry and I set off in the jeep to contact the police and Field Security Sections in the region. This investigation, the mystery of flashing lights at night and two inexplicable explosions uncomfortably close to Tac occupied us for the next two days, but none of these mysteries was solved as we had to pack for the move to our next location, Zonhoven in Belgium.

10
BACK IN BELGIUM

At the onset of winter our camp in the Eindhoven municipal gardens was cold and damp, and life in the tent was becoming uncomfortable. We could get up in the early morning to find our tents completely submerged beneath a sea of fog. Another reason for moving was that the front line of the army group was now facing east. The headquarters needed to have a position nearer to the centre, not so far north and looking towards the Rhine.

The move was carried out at night, in great secrecy, as part of an elaborate plan of deception. Private soldiers disguised as high ranking officers with red hat bands drove up in large staff cars to the Eindhoven site where a small rearguard still remained, while Tac HQ moved out, minus all signs. The main column arrived in Zonhoven at 2 a.m. on a bleak, rainy morning.

Zonhoven, a few miles from Hasselt (where Dirck groaned when they brought the good news from Ghent to Aix) was a melancholy place surrounded by flat, water-logged fields. Our first sight of the village, a single street of unprepossessing red brick houses, was not encouraging. By some uncanny conjunction of circumstances it was in this place that bad news, accidents, personal tragedies and the weather all conspired to confirm this first impression.

It was while we were stationed in Zonhoven that German Panzer Armies under the command of General Rundstedt made a last mighty effort to push the Allies back into the sea. It was from here that on the night of 18 December Field Marshal Montgomery was called away by a telephone message from General Eisenhower to take command of the

First and Ninth American Armies in the main Ardennes battle area. And so while we were in this village we became aware of a growing nervousness among the civilian population about the possible return of the Germans and a slight cooling of their enthusiasm for us.

It was here too that the flying bombs became a nightly menace, as Zonhoven was on direct line to Antwerp for certain V1 sites. It was a kind of buzz-bomb alley. On a visit to Hasselt I had my first view of the devastation caused by flying bombs, a sight all the more worrying when news came of this same threat to London.

It was in our sad village street that one of our lorries crushed to death a four-year-old boy; and in the grey, damp cemetery of Zonhoven that a nineteen-year-old Londoner, Private Clarke of the Defence Company, was buried in an army blanket. He died as a result of drinking the local spirits, one of the unacceptable faces of the liberation in the form of wood alcohol, considered suitable (by profiteers or collaborators?) for welcoming the visiting troops. I remembered that when we were in Normandy young Private Clarke, eager to give his sister a happy surprise for her wedding, had enlisted the help of Madame Hamel to choose a bridal dress in Bayeux.

Even a short trip to Brussels, from which the first liberation hysteria had departed, failed to dispel the gloom. In a jeweller's shop I bought earrings for my mother and happened to mention the liberation to the assistant who served me.

'Don't talk to me about the liberation,' she said.

I replied rather sharply:

'What have you got against the liberation?'

Realising the significance to me of her outburst, she explained:

'On the day of liberation I went out with my little daughter and my sister to greet the Tommies who were driving in triumphal procession through Brussels. Everyone was on the streets or at their balconies waving and cheering.

107

Someone in the crowd gave my little girl a bouquet to present to the soldiers in one of the leading tanks. As the child was lifted up to offer her flowers to the driver a Nazi sympathiser threw a grenade which killed my sister, and injured my daughter, while I lost the sight of one eye.'

After hearing this story I apologised for my own reaction to her earlier remark and enquired after her daughter. The child, though badly injured, was slowly recovering from the shock. The woman was permanently blind in one eye. She expressed more hatred of the Belgian Nazis than of the German variety.

'At least the latter are not traitors,' she said. 'Mais je les hais tous.' (But I hate them all.)

There seemed to be no end to the sadness.

In Zonhoven we were to spend the hardest winter of the war, snow-bound and with chains on the wheels of our vehicles as a precaution against skidding on the glassy surface of the roads. Winter had truly arrived, with frost, extreme cold, fog and icy winds. Life here was made more spartan for soldiers and civilians alike by electricity cuts and a serious shortage of coal. We spent hours manufacturing fuel bricks out of cement and coal dust. I would be in the middle of writing a report when we were suddenly plunged into darkness.

This was the first time that the whole of Tactical Headquarters had ever been put up in houses, a difficult operation with the steady increase in our numbers. I knew no Flemish and I discovered that with some families I made more headway in German than in French when trying to find billets for the men. (The Dutch had never allowed me to speak German). Gerry and I had a room above a butcher's shop: the stairs went up through a trap-door in the ceiling, so we had to be careful when getting out of our beds in the dark mornings not to fall through the hole. We spent the first morning fixing up our tent and flysheet over the outhouses to provide cover for our transport. We were glad to have a solid roof over our heads when we woke up to the first snow of that bitter season, then to be invited to a surprise breakfast of black pudding with the butcher's family.

Among other hardships suffered by the army at that time was the strike of Belgian railway workers which threatened to halt the flow of war *matériel* to the allied front. This became particularly noticeable in Zonhoven as this once sleepy village was now a highway for military traffic. The sounds of battle, sometimes distant, sometimes near, kept the population alert with persistent rumours of imminent enemy attack or the real experience of German air raids on this main artery of supply, and the occasional daredevil, low-flying, machine-gunning bomber or fighter plane.

The security of Tactical Headquarters during what remained of our stay in the Low Countries, while the progress of the Allies was halted in the Ardennes and the Russians were fighting in a life and death struggle on the snowbound eastern front, consisted of the usual routine duties, jerked momentarily into frantic action by some alarming report or startling discovery. There was continual surveillance of occasionally suspect but generally innocent civilians and, on the other hand, the sudden confrontation with five German soldiers hiding in the cellar of the café. They were arrested and transported to the nearest POW camp. The café owners were also apprehended to face judgment in the civil courts.

There were investigations of breaches of security by our own troops and, more seriously, a case of sabotage at the railhead from which *matériel* was destined for transport to the Front. Five men were arrested and brought back to the police station in Zonhoven. Late that night we searched the house of one suspect and had a harrowing time with his mother, whose high-pitched screams disturbed the neighbourhood. With loud, hysterical cries she implored us to spare her son.

I was up early the next morning preparing a report on the previous night's activities. Completing this, I then took the five suspects under escort by the Defence Company to Counter-Intelligence at Corps Headquarters for further interrogation.

More German soldiers were falling into our hands. Seven had to be interrogated, guarded and escorted, then two more came out of hiding. Who was giving them shelter? As there seemed to be some enemy-inspired activity in our area I drove the jeep to Bourg Léopold to question a German in the POW camp there who was a possible supplier of information. It was he who indicated where other Germans could be hiding, but no Belgian family was involved. His compatriots were in the open, in woods from which they would be driven out by the severe cold. All our German captives had a considerable growth of beard, so it did not look as if anyone had been sheltering them. All seemed to be thoroughly disillusioned – yet it was at this time, in the depths of winter, that the Germans launched their big offensive.

Early in December, while we were engrossed with the idea of hiding-places, the local partisans set us a test, to see if we could find theirs. It was so well hidden that it kept the Gestapo guessing all through the occupation. Members of the Resistance on the run were traced to the village, would be seen entering a house, and then their pursuers lost the scent. The fugitives had completely disappeared. A group of us were invited to search the house but we could not find the hiding-place. It was finally revealed to us in the thickness of a wall. The person hiding climbed up to the level of the first floor then stood on the trap door in the ceiling which gave entrance to the hiding-place. It was impossible to lift this trap door from below with someone standing on it, and it was camouflaged to look like the other ceilings in the house. There had been some narrow escapes but none of their friends had been caught.

For several days my own rôle was that of pursuer, in a round-up of collaborators, in a search for an illegal radio transmitter, and in yet another hunt after doubtful pigeons. All these assignments involved journeys into Hasselt to other Field Security (FS) Sections, to the *Sûreté*, the *Palais de Justice*, and the prison. The collaborators were dealt with by the FS Section in whose area they were found. I located the forbidden radio transmitter in the ruins of Kapellstraat. At the town hall I was given a list of a large number of pigeon-owners and then had to 'clear' them from the security point of view. After clambering in and out of innumerable pigeon lofts I was able to establish the innocence of what seemed to be several hundred pigeons, none of whom were obvious Nazi or Allied sympathisers but all strictly neutral and wanting, sensibly, to be left in peace.

One of my journeys into Hasselt in the cause of security took me to the Convent of the Ursulines. I had heard that in this predominantly Belgian and French community there were two English nuns who had been victims of reprisals during the occupation. I was anxious to hear their story and, though this was an enclosed order, the Mother Superior, in her concern for the two women, seemed equally interested for one of their compatriots to meet them.

The Mother Superior left me in the quiet convent parlour and after a few minutes the two women came in. This was still the era when the nun's habit was all-enveloping, from starched wimple to voluminous floor-sweeping skirt. Mère Majella was a small frail-looking woman, probably in her fifties, and Mère Ursule, taller and younger, possibly in her thirties.

We were soon deep in conversation, in French, because for so many years (Mère Majella had been in the convent from the age of eighteen) they had neither heard or spoken any English; even the radio had been denied them. Mère Majella had grown up in Haretown, my own home town while Mère Ursule was from Burslem. The Superior of the convent had given me the general outline of their story. It was left to the two women to fill in the details.

In 1940 an Allied bomber was shot down over Hasselt and all the crew were killed. At the burial in the local cemetery the whole town turned out, with prayers and hymns and flowers. Troops from the SS barracks, interpreting the long procession of mourners as a hostile demonstration, then surrounded the area and began to sort the people out for reprisals, which took the form of public floggings. As the church and convent figured conspicuously

111

in the service of respect paid to the dead airmen, the Mother Superior and her nuns were among the first targets of Nazi wrath. The two English nuns, in an attempt to spare their sisters, decided to give themselves up and declare their nationality. 'Punish us instead' was their plea.

As a result of this the two nuns were arrested, taken away to Bourg Léopold, the Belgian Aldershot, and placed in a kind of cage in the middle of the barrack square. Humiliation and ridicule were the main instruments of torture: as, for example, when they were given razors, shaving brushes and soap and made to shave their heads in full view of the jeering men. They had spent four years of the Nazi occupation in captivity. Mentally they had somehow survived this treatment, asking for God's blessing on their torturers, but physically they weakened almost to the point of collapse. Mère Ursule started to lose her teeth and her hair and they were saved only by the liberation; just to be taken back to the enclosed life of the convent. There was no trace of bitterness in either their voices or their faces, but disappointment when they said how sorry they were to have 'missed the liberation'. I was the first British soldier they had seen. It was understandable, therefore, that in view of all their sufferings the Mother Superior should see fit to relax the rule of the order to allow the two nuns to entertain an English guest.

I became a regular visitor to the convent and at one of my meetings with the nuns they asked if they could do some washing for me and for my friends. This would be shared out among the whole community. A few days later I arrived with a large bundle and on subsequent visits was startled to see long lines of men's socks, vests and underpants strung across the cloister. This work for the cause of victory seemed to give them great happiness. Perhaps there was some kind of mutual exchange. I had had my first glimpse of enclosed nuns and they were given an intimate view of the army. We were pleased to receive our clothes back unrecognisably immaculate, and our convent friends were delighted with our parcels of tea, sugar and margarine.

These journeys on the snow-muffled road to Hasselt were a welcome relief from the drabness of Zonhoven. Apart from the trip to Brussels, I was reminded again of Robert Browning when I spent a day's leave in beautiful Ghent, going duty-bound to Aerschot (where 'up leaped of a sudden the sun') and entered Germany for the first time on a visit to Aachen (Aix), which involved passing through the Siegfried Line. Travelling through Huy on another assignment in the Ardennes I appreciated the undulating country, so different from the flat landscapes of Eindhoven and Zonhoven, but signs of the recent fierce battle disfigured the Bastogne road where the bodies of dead Americans were still lying in the snow.

My diary during this time reflects an incongruous mixture of military pressures, civilian miseries and light-hearted relaxations. The events of a single day could transport us from darkness to light and back again. This was inevitable when one considered the war and Christmas coinciding in men's hearts and minds. Old men were spreading out their maps in centrally heated offices while young men were lying face down in the snow. We were taking prisoners and putting up Christmas decorations at the same time. One of the cruellest contrasts of all came on Sunday 17 December as I was playing the organ for the carol service. Monty was there and read the lesson; we had a pre-recording of the carols for the Christmas Eve BBC broadcast and photographs were taken. I stayed behind to hear the play-back, but was called out in the middle of the recording to speak to the grief-stricken mother of the four-year-old boy who had just been knocked down by one of our lorries and killed.

Tragedy was one aspect of army life, boredom was another. Acutely aware of this the official Entertainments Administration at Main Headquarters were particularly busy at times of stalemate, as they were at times of victory and celebration. Intense wintry weather belonged to a category of its own especially in a place where even the petrol froze. So in Zonhoven, for ever associated in my mind

113

with ice and snow and home-made briquettes, we were given a Variety Concert by Carroll Levis and his Discoveries.

More light-heartedness came with the Feast of St Nicholas, in which civilians and military joined together. On 5 December Steve and I bought Christmas cards in Hasselt as the local people made their preparations for St Nicholas' Day, then visited our two English nun friends at the Ursulines' Convent. They gave us soup, coffee and *spéculations* (gingerbread hearts) for this special feast.

On 6 December I watched the village procession of children, headed by St Nicholas and his assistant Black Peter with his sack for carrying off naughty boys and girls; back at the office we were given more *spéculations* by Madame Putman, and at the billet by my landlady. These cakes are made of wheat flour and honey, and are of various shapes: people, windmills, cockerels and bunches of grapes as well as hearts.

Though we were still involved with German prisoners and one Fascist activist in the *Jeunesse Flamande*, the spirit of Christmas was beginning to win through and claim more of our attention. The Battle of the Ardennes was still raging, but at the same time I was collecting Christmas trees from the priest in the village, playing the piano for our concert in the YMCA, sticking paper stars on the walls and ceiling of the Sergeants' Mess and attending the party which we gave for the children in the afternoon. They were shown five cartoon films, had tea, and each child received a present. Lieutenant James of our MT Section was appropriately fitted out as St Nicholas to three hundred and thirty-five children. I found time to go into Hasselt to buy a Christmas present for Madame Putman, to have tea with the nuns and to hitch-hike back.

On Christmas Eve I received the news that I was due for leave on 3 January (the first since before D-Day) and with the joy of my own 'release' could not help being aware of the irony of taking yet more German soldiers into custody.

Though present at the pre-recording on 17 December, Monty had to miss the actual Carol Service broadcast on Christmas

Eve from our Tac HQ to take charge against the serious counter-offensive launched by the Germans in the Ardennes. We were able to listen to our own carols and Monty's Christmas message at 8 p.m. that evening on the wireless. In Zonhoven everything stopped for Christmas. I played the piano for a lively sing-song in the Sergeants' Mess and at 10 p.m. at a party at Putman's I made a speech and presented a table lamp and a box of chocolates to Madame Putman.

The party broke up at 5.30 a.m. but I somehow got up early enough to go to church parade in the YMCA canteen. This was followed by Holy Communion. Monty gave an address between the two services, during which he told us that he once more commanded the British and American forces of the northern sector. The German counter-attack was a serious one and the Americans had suffered heavy losses, but no decision had yet been made to cancel our leave.

CHRISTMAS DAY

There was no offensive from the British side on Christmas Day. The British Army in Zonhoven celebrated Christmas in traditional style with an ENSA concert in the afternoon, then Christmas cake and mince pies for tea. Dinner was at 8 o'clock in the evening with turkey, goose, pork chop, Brussels sprouts, baked potatoes, Yorkshire pudding, red wine, Christmas pudding, mince pies, oranges, beer, whisky and cigars. We had a sing-song for which I played the piano ('Bless 'em all', 'I've got sixpence', 'Roll out the barrel', 'Kiss me good-night sergeant-major' . . .). Nearly everybody was tight and Butch did a striptease.

Was there a trace of hysteria in our merrymaking? These men had been herded together for seven or eight months in isolated places with no sight or sound of home and family. Now we were promised leave, and this was Christmas Day. The lid was off.

As civilians most of us must have tried, however obscurely, to make life meaningful for ourselves and I, as a teacher, had struggled, often despairingly, to do the same for children. The war changed all that. In the army, digging antiquated trenches with pick and shovel in the Royal Engineers, and Tac HQ chasing pigeons and getting people locked up, did not come across to me as meaningful activities. Yet in the soldier's life there were hidden gains unsuspected by me at the time. These came from the disciplines, the excitements, the irksomeness, the adventures, the endurances and the hazards shared with others from many different walks of life. Looking back, these are experiences I would not now want to be without.

There were other bonuses too, related to the job itself. I began to have the strange impression that in spite of impaired hearing I was developing a greater sensitivity to different sounds, just as in visual awareness I was becoming acutely alert to unusual or altered features of the environment. This included everyday sounds, from the rattle of the Belgian trams with their loud gong-like horns, and the bell in the butcher's shop when anybody entered, to the sinister motorbike noise of the flying bombs and even the special quality of the silence preceding the explosion. I imagined that civilian policemen might develop these peculiar sharpnesses of hearing and vision in the course of a lifetime spent in purposeful listening and looking.

Acute hearing was not needed on 31 December when the whole countryside trembled under the roar of over one hundred bombers heading south. The situation in the Ardennes was becoming critical and great concern was being openly expressed by local people. At midnight dark-haired Sergeant Nicholson brought the New Year in with him. We sang 'Auld Lang Syne', drank a toast and had dances with everybody decorating each other: 1945 – would this be the year of the peace?

Back at the billet I sorted out my kit for going on leave. Among my things I packed a certificate. At the conclusion of church parade Monty had made a presentation to myself and four others. He thanked us and shook hands. So perhaps pigeon-hunting was not such a bore after all?

11

ON LEAVE

1945

My long-awaited seven days' leave took me into another world, but not all at once. There was the blancoing and packing, the visit to the MO, the collecting of passes, rations and ration cards, the journey by 15 cwt truck to the first Transit Camp where instructions were given through loudspeakers, the march in three ranks in the darkness across bomb-pitted ground to the troop carriers which took us on our bumpy way to the waiting trains. These had no heating and no lighting. My train was due to leave at 6.53 p.m. but it was 9 p.m. before we moved off. Stiff with cold, I spent the time gazing out of the window watching engines shunting. After what seemed an endless journey, stopping at many stations, we arrived at Lille at 8 o'clock the next morning. Here we had tea and sandwiches then climbed back into the train for Calais which we reached at 11.45 a.m. Here we had dinner, changed our money, received our embarkation tickets, had a wash, then stood round the stove in a Nissen hut until it was time to move off to the boat which was due to sail at 6. p.m. A band was playing for us on the quayside but they were shivering in the icy wind, and a sheet of music was blown into the water.

I spent the whole of the boat trip on the top deck, staring at the stars, watching the French coast out of sight, then looking at the lights of Dover – I was very sick.

By comparison with the French train the Southern Railway was comfortable and warm. I enjoyed a cup of coffee at the NAAFI on the train and arrived at Victoria at

10.45 p.m. An explosion at Sloane Square Underground Station reminded me that I had not left the war behind.

My father was waiting for me as I arrived at Sudbury Hill Station at 11.30 p.m. He had been there since 8 p.m., clad in overcoat and mac. Mother, waiting at home, produced a wonderful supper of eggs and bacon and we talked until the early hours. It was breakfast in bed, every soldier's dream, then began a round of meetings and visits with friends and relations. At home there were long chats by the fire, Christmas pudding and cake, mince pies, nuts, sweets and apples. The street lighting was on again and windows were no longer blacked-out but dimmed.

On Friday 12 January, the last day of my leave, we had a big 'Sunday' dinner of roast lamb, then a few hours later, after a supper of fried eggs and spam in the front room, I packed my kit and said my goodbyes to face the bleak journey back to Germany. My mother and father saw me off at Victoria where I met one of my returning friends. At 1.30 a.m. we piled on to trucks at Dover Priory and were taken to barracks where we spent the night, first queueing in the dark and the bitter cold for tea and the exchange of money, then sleeping for about two hours. We breakfasted and drew a blanket each. Lorries took us down to the boat station for a long wait in the cold and dark. We embarked as it gradually grew lighter. We reached Calais at 11 a.m., 13 January then went by train to the Transit Camp where we were issued with rail and meal tickets. We joined another queue for dinner but, though I had not been sick on this return journey, I only had an appetite for peaches, cream and tea. We were here long enough to have a wash and see a film, Olivia de Havilland in *Government Girl*. For this we stood on a plank balanced on petrol tins at the back of a large audience of servicemen.

We queued up for tea which was served by French civilians, then queued up for the train which at last left Calais at 6 p.m. With no heating or lighting and sitting on a wooden seat I was grateful to wrap myself in the blanket against the cold and the lack of upholstery. We reached Lille at 9.30 p.m. then queued up for a cooked meal which we ate at tables on the station platform where large coke braziers had been placed at intervals between piles of snow. We left shortly after 10 p.m. and I eventually went to sleep in the train, waking up on arrival at Bourg Léopold where we had breakfast and were waited on by Belgian civilians. We collected our own party together and stood round one of the fires until a driver from Tac arrived at noon to take us back to camp. The truck skidded several times on the frozen road and it was a relief when we finally reached Zonhoven. I had dinner in the mess, unpacked, washed, shaved and gave Bob Forrest the mince pie from his mother, whom I had met while on leave. At 'tea-time' I had coffee, pâté and a Belgian waffle in my billet at Madame Schepers' butcher's shop, then went to bed at 5.45 p.m.

12

THE GERMAN COLLAPSE

Life in the Section had changed during my absence on leave. The captain had left to join the Second Armoured Division and I found myself involved in the usual check on buildings and billets for documents left behind in our imminent move to a new location. This was Geldrop, the Golden Village.

We were into February and a thaw had transformed Zonhoven from a snowbound wilderness into an island in a sea of mud. It was against this that our vehicles had to struggle on their way out on to the familiar road to Holland. Accommodation for our headquarters, expanded now by the addition of extra Sappers and Signalmen, was in factories and private houses. I was billeted with a young married couple who made me welcome with a cup of tea. I was very conscious of my battledress caked in mud as they showed me my immaculately clean bedroom. In spite of the comfort of these new lodgings sleep was impossible because of the ceaseless drone of bombers which marked our relentless assault on the Reich. Geldrop was a pleasant place and spirits rose with the approach of spring. The large, vivacious Padding family kept an ever-open door for our section, with lively talk, cups of coffee and evenings spent in teasing, laughter and musical games. Next door to them lived quiet gentle Maria, a civilising influence in those convulsive days. Our soujourn here was all too brief, but there was plenty of work for the whole section. One of our main jobs on this industrial site was to vet the factory-workers, compile a list of names and stand by while they signed on each morning.

News of big Russian gains in the east began to coincide with the acceleration of our own advance in the west, and eventually with an ever-quickening pace we found ourselves, after another short stop on a war-ravaged heathland site above Venlo, approaching the Rhine and racing through Germany.

In this sad country we found destruction on a vast scale. Travelling along the bomb-scarred roads involved detours through adjacent fields and over flattened walls of collapsed buildings. Some of these were churches, and through the chaotic labyrinth of Münster our tyres and tank tracks crunched and pulverised the carved stone faces and limbs of medieval statues. Saints and angels destined by their artists for the pinnacles of Münster Cathedral now lay broken in the dust, soon to be churned into mud by the heavy spring rains. Houses, too many to number, had been smashed by our bombers and those not destroyed lay wide open with their furniture and other contents scattered across the congested roads. Grimness was everywhere: in the wasted countryside, in the despoiled towns and in the gaunt faces of the people.

It was in Germany, at Straelen, that Tac HQ took to the woods. Our security rôle in Germany was to be totally different from that in France and the Low Countries. There we had been working with a civilian majority against a minority of collaborators, desperado snipers or saboteurs. Here everyone was a potential enemy, and in spite of the general disillusion with the failing fortunes of their own war effort there was for us always the danger of a German ambush or booby trap, one of the favourite ones being a steel wire stretched tightly across the road at neck level to decapitate allied motor cyclists. These were realities against which we needed to be constantly on guard.

At one of our woodland sites the Counter-Intelligence Detachment settled for a few days in a deserted house, possibly once the home of a forester. In this twilight environment we spent our first days searching for the German soldiers' hideouts for which these woods were notorious. Our few successes involved escorting despondent German deserters to the nearest POW camp.

Already warmer weather added to the hopes of an end to the war and made us go about our work with cheerfulness in spite of the desolation, the misery and the struggle so visible and tangible beyond our own cosy perimeter. Catkins and palm were in blossom on trees and hedgerows. The morning and afternoon sun began to dry the February mud and the evening sky had a warm bluish glow evocative of spring. On one of these bright sunny mornings I picked up the telephone to hear the following message from one of the sentries: 'Mabel is here. Will you come and sign for her. She's for the Chief and will need an escort.' It was most unusual in this all-male and almost monastic establishment to receive such a call. Who was Mabel, and what was she supposed to be doing here? This was one aspect of Monty's character with which I was unacquainted. Consumed with curiosity I rushed to greet the newcomer. Mabel had four legs and turned out to be a cow, requisitioned by one of the ADCs to supply the Chief with a ready supply of fresh milk. So Mabel was to join the rest of the menagerie which included the two dogs, named 'Hitler' and 'Rommel', a horse which had belonged to Rommel, an aviary of budgerigars and other birds and an aquarium of tropical fish. The sheep had not yet arrived. Swans, cygnets and a peacock arrived later to grace our peace-time headquarters.

A wide anti-tank ditch ran through our camp, and there were many well-made dug-outs in the woods – possibly part of the Siegfried Line defences. As the fine weather continued the roar of the bombers grew louder and more prolonged. Rumours about German deserters persisted and we continued to scour the woods and carry out house searches. Some German youths, disenchanted with their own war prospects, even undertook to show us German ammunition and anti-tank weapons concealed in the woods.

The big Allied offensive preceding the Rhine crossing began during the night of 23 March. The continuous noise of the bombers kept us awake and, getting up to watch, we could discern their dark shapes moving in a steady flow over the trees. The next morning Major Odgers read to the assembled camp a message from the Chief announcing the all-out push of the Allies across the Rhine into the heart of Germany.

On Sunday 25 March we all turned out for a special Church Parade at which the Commander-in-Chief and the Prime Minister were both present. There was a presentation of four certificates and in his address the Prime Minister said:

'If I had been asked in 1940 how we were to defeat Germany I should not have known what to say.'

He spoke with unbounded confidence, as if that defeat were already an accomplished fact.

Events were certainly moving towards a climax and the skies above Germany were full of activity, humming with the continual traffic of aircraft. During the night, while standing-by in the office, I watched ack-ack tracer shells pursuing enemy planes.

At our little house in the woods we took it in turns to do the daily domestic duties: preparing the fire for the sharing water, getting breakfast, washing up and doing the laundry in the ancient, rusty copper now that we were miles from the friendly Belgian nuns and Dutch ladies who used to do this for us.

Firelighting with petrol is highly dangerous, strictly illegal and was totally at variance with my early training as a Boy Scout. Our method was to scrape together a small patch of sandy soil, soak it with a few drops of petrol from a jerrycan and throw a lighted match on to it. The result was a lively flame which burned fiercely and long enough to boil our shaving water.

On the morning of 27 March I got up early to light the fire in the small clearing behind the house. I tilted the full jerrycan to pour some of its contents on the ground, not realising that it was still hot from a fire recently lit by someone who had got up even earlier. Immediately a wall of flame ran up the stream of petrol, engulfing me and the can I was holding. My trousers were on fire and I spent some frantic minutes beating out the flames, then as the jerrycan burst open with a loud explosion I saw to my horror a lake of fire spreading towards our jeep with its full cargo of jerrycans loaded in readiness for our departure that day. Having managed to extinguish the flames on my clothing I jumped into the jeep and reversed it madly out of reach of the advancing inferno which was now licking the branches of nearby trees. Thoughts of a forest fire and the knowledge that only fifty yards away in that same forest were the C-in-C, his staff and all our war-time plans and hopes, made me leap hither and thither, snatching at branches already well alight, tearing them down and stamping on them until the last flickerings had died away in spirals of thick smoke. On the ground the fiery flood was almost touching the wall of the house. Running for the spade I worked and sweated (as much with fright as with the effort) until I had smothered the last waves of that angry tide with earth.

The time was 6 a.m. Half an hour later the rest of the section got up, oblivious of the traumas through which I had just passed; the fire was out, the last embers stifled underneath shovelsful of sand and earth. The early riser came back through the woods and asked me if I had noticed anything strange, as he had seen from the distance a brilliant glow in the direction of our house and what looked like someone doing a war dance.

I was slow to learn my lesson from that experience: the very next day, I blew the doors off our stove by trying to coax the few dying sparks with a drop of petrol. This caused a column of flame to explode vertically up the chimney and a tongue of fire to shoot horizontally into our tiny kitchen. From that day onwards I have been very wary of playing with fire and respectful of the power of petrol.

The 27th was the day when we should have moved off, as we were already packed to go with the advance party. We did set off but were jammed in a record-breaking traffic block which we were told stretched for fifteen miles. We had to return to our cottage in the woods. While our convoy was stuck in the procession I cut up cheese sandwiches because we were too late for dinner. As it was my turn for domestic duties I made the tea on our return and decided to do the laundry.

On 28 March we set off again for a new position nearer the Rhine at Bonninghardt, having been warned by the Camp Commandant that the district was heavily mined. On arrival at our destination we established ourselves in an empty farmhouse. All the houses we entered had a similar smell, sweetly stale. Routine searches revealed hidden rifles on the farm, discoveries which we reported to the Military Government, but the bürgermeister was nowhere to be found. At 6 p.m. we heard the news on the wireless that the German army was disintegrating. This fact was borne out by the number of German deserters who approached us with white flags.

At night we saw flashes of gunfire along the Rhine front. There were other disturbances during the hours of darkness, the banging of shutters and the sound of footsteps near the house. Investigation showed the intruders to be cows, possibly seeking the absent farmer. In the morning we were awakened by other country sounds – the crowing of the rooster and the working of the pump handle.

We moved on again, crossing the Rhine on three pontoon bridges. The waste of war was all about us: dead horses, dead cows and even more dead German soldiers. We saw gliders lying in great profusion in the fields on the east bank of the Rhine beyond Wesel and large numbers of German prisoners of war by the roadside. On our speedy return to report back to the main body of Tac HQ we were called to investigate a light in the farm behind our house and found two German soldiers in hiding there.

Back again at the new location at Brunen we encountered two German soldiers walking down the road with a white flag and a safe-conduct pass. They gave themselves up to us and I marched them down to the CMP Post where we interrogated and searched them. Ken went back with one of them to recover their weapons which they had hidden. The other one spoke to me and said there was nothing now between us and Berlin: the German soldiers would not fight any more, officers were abandoning their men and Germany was finished. He had a fiancée in Cologne and was anxious to get back home. I took both men to the POW camp where there were many prisoners and displaced persons, French, Belgians and Russians.

Our days were a mixture of deprivations and excitements, but the nights were alight with the brilliance of searchlights, flares, fires and tracers over the Rhine. On 31 March the main body of Tac HQ crossed the Rhine by a floating bridge at Wesel. We found ourselves back in tents again, in a dell on the edge of a forest.

The 1 April was a Sunday and Monty, never deflected from his commitment to regular religious observance, arranged for the headquarters to celebrate Matins and Holy Communion in a barn. Later we were to have a mobile church, reminiscent of the Ark of the Covenant which accompanied and comforted the Israelites on their long journey in the wilderness.

We put our watches on to double summer time. Was this why we had resumed life under canvas? Had bureaucracy decreed: 'This is summer, and summer means canvas, ground sheets and sore knees?' We were moving with such speed through Germany that we were never far from the front line and were soon to run into danger. We were encountering abandoned German military establishments, barracks, dug-outs and searchlight batteries full of jettisoned equipment: guns, ammunition, picks, shovels and mallets. The tail fins of bombs scattered over the fields told their own story of the magnitude of the Allied air attack.

On the move to Nottuln our convoy passed through crowds of liberated French prisoners. We were surprised to find the village people smiling at us and generally looking relieved. In our efforts to establish a camp site they were prompt to cooperate, and the few local inhabitants with whom we were obliged to communicate in those non-fraternising days were not slow to profess their dislike of the Nazis.

Here we found the houses full of evacuees and among them two children with scarlet fever. We saw the local doctor and I travelled in his car to arrange for them to be taken to the hospital. He spoke French, perhaps imagining that it would be distasteful to me for the conversation to be in German, and said that the villagers were glad to be liberated (his own words), though his wife thought I had come to arrest him. He insisted that ninety per cent of his patients were anti-Nazi. In spite of his professed Allied sympathies the doctor had a cache of rifles in his house which Ken and I confiscated. In the hospital we saw and checked twenty wounded members of the Wehrmacht, four of whom were women. We also paid a visit to the underground tunnels of the Wehrkreis, then to a farm where Polish workers were reported to have threatened to murder the German family. The farmer's wife thanked us for 'liberating' them and gave us eggs and apples.

After the briefest of stays the advance party was on the move again. This meant an early start soon after 6 a.m. We packed and loaded the jeep and set off. The devastated centre of Münster was still burning and the consequences of the bombing in human terms were everywhere to be seen throughout the country and on the roads in the long, slow-moving processions of refugees. At Rheine, our new location, we discovered that twenty-seven people were living at the home of the local doctor, who requested that they be allowed to stay there. With so many shattered houses and huge numbers of displaced people looking for shelter it was not only humane but reasonable to allow them to stay. One woman was terrified that the German army would return to the village; this was strange since such an event would obviously mean a successful change in their own military fortunes. Such was the confusion in the minds and emotions of civilians that we found resignation along with resentment, and arrogance mixed with envy. I spoke to German prisoners who expressed relief at being captured. There were traces of grim humour and self-mockery, but remorse was totally lacking in their conversation and demeanour.

Among civilians the one dominant feeling was fear of the

Russians. In view of the tremendous cost in Russian lives resulting from Hitler's invasion of the Soviet Union, they had reason to fear. We were now entering a phase where we had to deal with raiding parties of Russians armed with revolvers and rifles, seeking to revenge themselves on German families on whose estates they had served sentences of slave labour. Little did we think that on entering enemy territory we should be required to assume the rôle of protectors. Military Police functioned in the towns with the willing or reluctant help of the remaining forces of law and order, but in the country all was anarchy, chaos and fear of marauding Russians and Poles.

In this atmosphere of misery we came upon a nightmare landscape of industrial ruins, burnt-out buildings and twisted, broken railway lines with water and bomb craters everywhere. When we walked we sank over our ankles into mud. Our first sight of jet aircraft (a German bomber which drew fire from our ground artillery) elicited from Tony the remark that he was frightened of the future with its threat of unimaginable violence.

We spent the night of 7 April in an empty German barracks, eerie with the smell of decay and death. One room was like a charnel-house; the floor was covered with what looked like charred bones, misshapen and almost liquefied by intense heat. Our joint feeling of horror at this dreadful place, with its giant slogans preaching sacrifice and obedience (*Gehorsam*), was given substance when our Medical Officer verified the presence of burnt human remains in that derelict barrack room.

A Russian ex-officer, accompanied by a Pole, reported to us the existence of a group of SS men and other Nazi Party members still in the town (Osnabrück). Our two informers fixed a rendezvous with us at the chalk-pits but our first efforts to hunt down the SS proved to be fruitless. In view of the threat which desperate men might present to the headquarters it was important to continue the search. As a result of this and with the help of our Russian friend we did run one SS man to earth and escorted him to 309 Field Security Section in Neuenkirchen. His companions had departed at the approach of the Allied armies.

On 9 April, with feelings of relief, our advance party left those gruesome barracks for what was to be the most idyllic resting place of our whole odyssey. On our long journey to Ostenwalde we crossed the dried-up Dortmund–Ems Canal. We were greeted along the road by crowds of liberated prisoners of war: Poles, French, Russians and Yugoslavs. The latter were particularly boisterous in their greetings, laughingly obliging us to stop, gripping us with both hands and putting their arms round our shoulders. Trying to make some kind of reciprocal gesture of comradeship I gave a packet of cigarettes to one of Tito's warriors. They wore grey, the Russians green, the French and Poles khaki. After this friendly exchange we were caught for hours in a long convoy and stopped for lengthy intervals.

Then after a tiring journey but on a beautiful spring day we first set eyes upon the enchantment that was the Schloss at Ostenwalde, home of Baron von Vincke, a cousin of Prince Bernhard of the Netherlands. The Commander-in-Chief was so entranced by his first sight of the Schloss that he stopped and announced:

'This is where I am going to live when we have won the war.'

Nestling in its Arcadian setting the building looked as if it had not been disturbed for centuries. The war seemed far away and the presence of our lorries and armoured vehicles was a brutal intrusion. The exterior was that of a comfortable, seventeenth-century manor house, and its interior an example of exquisite eighteenth-century taste in design and furniture. We wandered from room to room in breathless wonderment. There was the Mozartzimmer, the music room with its white grand piano, the Sonnenscheinzimmer, the Gartenzimmer, the library and, in the baroness's bedroom, a magnificent bed in the shape of a swan. All the furniture and draperies were immaculate.

Rich farm buildings with ample arched entrances stood on each side of the spacious lawn which sloped gently down to the Schloss, and massive timeless beeches lined the approach from the road. Gardens and a lake stretched behind the house to the extensive woods beyond. Both Melle, the nearest country town, and the neighbouring village of Oldendorf showed no outward signs of having been touched by the war. The whole of this rural area was an oasis of peace and beauty.

We pitched our tents in a nearby field and settled down there for the night, but were alerted by mysterious lights in the empty Schloss. Upon investigation we found that the generator, having been connected to the power supply, had caused some of the lights to go on inside the building.

We woke up to a beautiful spring morning with birds singing and bright sunshine streaming into the tent. We hung out our bedding to air, then made a thorough search of the barns and outbuildings and the Schloss. In the loft we found arms and radios, the latter requisitioned or confiscated from the Dutch.

After dinner two of us went to the Military Government to ascertain the exact nature of the baron's involvement, if any, with the Nazi Party. It was known that in his youth he had enjoyed the companionship of English friends. Another routine duty, part of our everyday life both in England and on the continent, was the eviction of trespassers from our camp precincts. This applied equally to former residents of the property and to casual visitors from outside. It was as if the Schloss were now ours, at least during the length of our stay. One of the resident farmers had to be restrained from encroaching on to the field where our tents were pitched. He was respectful of our orders, reviled Hitler and the Party and said he hoped his district would be governed by either the British or the Americans, but not by the Russians. He said that many Germans would welcome Montgomery as their new Führer. There might have been some truth in this statement, as we learned that another neighbouring farmer had been imprisoned by the Nazis for his political opinions.

The main body of Tac HQ arrived on 10 April. I had to requisition a roller for the airstrip which arrived drawn by two cows under the control of a Russian. I had to walk in front to show him the airstrip, and carried on a conversation over my shoulder. He said he did not want to return to Russia but would like to volunteer to stay in Germany. He wondered if this would be allowed by an 'English' government.

In the evening we called to see the baron in the local Gasthof. He spoke to us at the door with a lighted candle in his hand.

13

LOVE FROM RUSSIA

Fear and hate were the dominant emotions among the people we met on this part of our journey; they were some of the war's less spectacular disfigurements. There was no doubt that the Russians were greatly feared by the local population, and such was the hatred vented by the Russians upon their former captors that we were repeatedly called upon as arbitrators if not as peacemakers. This was a situation brought about by our own rapid advance, by the liberation of prison camps and by the ending of slave labour, which set free thousands of displaced persons who poured on to roads already clogged by military traffic. Among them were Russians and Poles seeking vengeance, some of them armed with weapons and ammunition taken from wrecked trains and deserted barracks. Added to these numbers were the homeless Germans 'displaced' by Allied bombing, and unhappy runaway soldiers. The sight of a dead person was always chilling, but the plight of the living wandering without hope through scenes of desolation was a long drawn-out nightmare.

These were the miseries that confronted us when we went outside the enchanted acres of Ostenwalde. We were continually being called away, not to investigate pigeons but to hunt after hidden or stolen arms and ammunition. Three Germans came to report that a group of sixty Russians had taken ammunition from a train and were terrorising the village. I telephoned Major Weaver, the officer in charge of the Defence Company and, using the three Germans as guides, he sent two armoured cars and a truckload of infantry to deal with the incident. They succeeded in disarming the Russians, who bore us no malice but on the

133

contrary were friendly, crowding round us to shake hands and embrace us with all the warmth due to allies and comrades. In the prevailing climate of resentment and distrust these brotherly gestures made a welcome change.

Not far from the train, which we searched for more arms and ammunition, was a camp in which we found a mixed population of Russians and Poles of all ages, as well as a few other nationalities. There were grey-haired old men, wrinkled elderly women, babes in arms, husky young men and women. Experiences of life under the Germans were simply and artlessly related, cigarettes distributed on our side, and small babies held up to be fondled and admired by the British liberators. There was no stopping the handshakes, the back-slappings and the V-signs. Almost as an afterthought two antique rifles were confiscated and our miniature expeditionary force set out to visit another Russian camp in a neighbouring village. Our escort was a dilapidated civilian German car crammed to bursting point with stalwart, smiling Soviets.

The reception given to us at this second camp was even warmer than at the first and our three German informers were crestfallen and bewildered spectators of a boisterous, international rally. Our British troopers from the turret of their armoured car had difficulty in discharging their disciplinary, restraining role when confronted by the ever-increasing tide of friendly Russians and Poles surging round them. Three Dutchmen in this garrulous, gesticulating crowd stood out by reason of their clean appearance. The Russians had a genius for simple friendliness, the marks of suffering and privation on their faces erased momentarily by broad, beaming smiles. Most of them could speak German and we were bombarded with questions. Many of the women wanted to know when they would be able to return to Russia. The men did not seem anxious to go home, but appeared to want to taste their new-found freedom in this foreign land which had claimed them for so long already. One girl asked us if we could provide soldiers to guard them as she was nervous of the Germans. So there was fear on both sides. We reassured her by saying that British troops were to be found everywhere in the vicinity and that the Germans were more scared of the Russians than of anything else. One of the Poles drew me aside, inviting me to join them on one of their nocturnal raids and promising:

'Much shooting, many corpses.'

Having no taste for corpses I changed the subject by saying:

'One of our men is a Pole.'

I looked round for Tony Posnansky, who had unfortunately disappeared. This gruesome invitation was not altogether without result. It did have the advantage of making us redouble our efforts to disarm potential raiders and amateur terrorists. Another resident at the camp, a Russian, had a long and obviously sad tale of suffering to tell. It was delivered in a soft, mysterious tone of voice, a little above a whisper, and was almost unintelligible except that at the end of every sentence the Russian said:

'Nicht gut ha?'

To which I replied:

'Nicht gut.' This went on like a litany. I would have liked to understand more and to react more meaningfully to what was clearly a painful story.

It was past 5 p.m. and there was a general move towards departure, but all that resulted was a reshuffling of groups who settled down once again to question, admire and reminisce. Eventually we departed with our three German guides but not before all those who called themselves Allies had been given, and accepted, a pressing invitation to celebrate the camp dwellers' liberation with a party that night. Our jeep was so overloaded that when it came to a bend in the road it failed to turn and shot off at a tangent across the ditch, which was fortunately bridged at that point by a narrow path. After that slight shock we were back on the road again and took our Germans to the airstrip where they had left their bicycles. They thanked us for our efforts at protection and went away with mystified expressions on their faces.

Later that evening as dusk was falling several jeep-loads of British soldiers made their way across the fertile country of Westphalia towards a small village where a tall factory chimney marked the home of an expectant band of displaced persons: Russians, Poles, Dutch and one Belgian girl from Ghent. They came out smiling to meet us. The party started with more talk on both sides, and threatened to develop into an open-air meeting until a move was made towards the huts where the workers had their sleeping quarters. They apologised for the absence of light and pressed us to sit down by the large stove which cast a red glow over the darkened dormitory. Double-decker beds stood in a long row by the wall. On one or two of these beds a dark shape lay huddled, and women in night attire shuffled unselfconsciously past us with curious glances. From a neighbouring room came sounds of music and stamping feet. We made our way through to where two girls with kerchiefs round their heads were dancing, arms akimbo, to the accompaniment of a balalaika while a large crowd looked on. This was followed by 'Tipperary' on the harmonica, an obvious cue for some Anglo-Saxon community singing. During this stage of the proceedings some of us noticed that Captain Thornton and Tony were missing. A Russian offered to escort me to where they were and led me off into the night to another factory three-quarters of a mile away. The night was dark, the road was lonely, the Russian spoke excellent German (an accomplishment invariably treated with suspicion by sensitive Intelligence-trained personnel), and I have to confess that even with my six rounds of .38 I felt uneasy until, on nearing the second tall factory chimney, I heard the strains of an ancient piano. Inside the hut from which these sounds came I found lights, women dancing and many members of our headquarters who looked flushed and merry. Among them were my 'missing' colleagues. It has to be remembered that at that uncertain time in Germany's history and in circumstances that can only be described as *louche*, any unexplained disappearance of a member of HM Forces was a cause of some anxiety. (At one of the German farms which we visited during our search for weapons a complete British uniform was found. Neither its previous owner nor an explanation was forthcoming).

I arrived just too late for this second party, which was breaking up. Among the workers here were a French couple who managed to look strangely out of place, but we had during our passage through France and Belgium met families whose relatives had been uprooted from their homes for slave labour in German factories. Fernand Gennotte had been one of these.

There was now a departure *en masse* for the first factory where the jeeps had been parked, but this was by no means the close of the evening's celebrations. In our absence a meal had been prepared and we were invited to sit down again. A clean, white cloth was thrown over the rough wooden table and we were regaled with fried German sausage, black bread and pancakes coated with sugar, the whole washed down with neat methylated spirits. The Russians stood all round the table urging us to drink and taking notice of our progress. It was as if they had thrown down a gauntlet and were challenging us to pick it up, to test our valour. In the midst of a toast to Stalin and Churchill I surreptitiously and unpatriotically exchanged my liquor for a nearby glass of water. Tony was not so lucky. Seeing him hesitate one of the Russians grabbed him by the neck while another tried to pour the fiery liquid down his throat. He clenched his teeth and the contents of the glass poured down his chin. This amounted to an insult not only to Churchill but to their own leader, Stalin. I tried to explain that Tony's religion forbade him to take strong drink and that no offence was intended. The night was now far spent and this seemed an appropriate moment for us to start going back to camp. Our hosts, still in festive mood, lined themselves up throughout the entire length of the barrack-like room towards the door and shook hands with each of us in turn. Thus passed one of the most pleasant evenings we had yet spent in Germany. We came back in the pitch dark night in a warm glow of friendly, international thoughts and feelings.

On 12 April we heard two important items of news: that the Americans had crossed the Elbe and that President Roosevelt had died.

We were soon to leave the green stillness of Ostenwalde to travel further into war-scarred Germany. The reconnaissance party left first and, for once, I was not with them. I spent most of the day enjoying the unaccustomed peace of the camp area, and the evening writing by candlelight in the tent.

On 13 April we were awakened as arranged at 6 a.m. but were not required to strike the tent; Captain Thornton, Ken and I were being left behind to check the baron's property. Among the orders issued on the departure from Ostenwalde was the following: 'All kits will be inspected for loot.' The three of us who were left behind went to the quaint, pretty village of Buer to return a trailer which had been borrowed from a farmer – his son spoke to us in fluent English. On the road we met a German prisoner of war who had been released by the Canadians as they had nowhere to keep him. He and two other German soldiers had made their own prisoner of war cage by taking over an empty cottage and surrounding it with barbed wire. They showed us their 'prison', then surrendered to us. We took them to the nearest orthodox POW camp.

Back at Ostenwalde we went for a walk in the evening and sat on the hill overlooking the camp. We had a panoramic view of the Schloss, the surrounding fields and the woods stretching into the distance. There was a gleam of camp fires and hurricane lamps in tents from which came bursts of laughter and singing. A few stars shone above the stately trees in a clear sky. With a little effort of imagination this could be Napoleon's army resting at Ostenwalde before the road to Moscow. Night made our camp anonymous and in some strange way timeless.

The next morning we packed our kit, struck the tent and loaded the jeeps and the 15 cwt truck in readiness for the move. The truck left with the main party. We stayed behind with some of the Defence Company until a search of the Schloss and the surrounding area had been made and the baron notified. We made a report then left.

The war soon caught up with us again after our brief respite. We were reminded of BBC news broadcasts announcing 'a thousand-bomber raid on Germany' as we, in common with other land forces, travelled through the battered targets of these attacks – the devastation was widespread. Soon after our arrival at the new site I went with Tony and Lieutenant White in the jeep to Neustadt and the heavily bombed town of Hannover. One of the objects of our journey was to find a house suitable for use as an officers' mess, but throughout the length and breadth of this vast metropolis we failed to find one that was habitable. We passed a wrecked trainload of V2 rockets near Nienburg; the railway cutting had been seared and prised wide open, either by aerial bombardment or by artillery on the ground. We then crossed the Weser at Stolzenau.

We had travelled fast and far in the last few days, and with the noise of battle all about us the nearness of the enemy was now more of a reality. I went on foot to collect provisions and came back in the moonlight to our lonely bivouac carrying tea, sugar, powdered milk and a loaf of bread in one hand and a loaded revolver in the other. I kept looking behind me as I passed the wood, an understandable reaction as our efforts to tighten the security of Tac HQ had been rewarded by the capture of four SS men on the run and by the discovery of a large collection of rifles and pistols from various farms. At Asendorf Captain Thornton and I visited the bürgermeister who surrendered all the arms that had been in his possession, and then I went to all the neighbouring farms with officers of the Defence Company in a continuing search for weapons. This was important in view of the number of German soldiers wandering and hiding in the countryside.

Heavy gunfire persisted throughout the day and night; I stayed up on guard. There was a lot of air activity and a great display of tracers. There were other strange noises nearer the ground, like footsteps over gravel, but I found that they came from the creaking beds as men turned over in their sleep.

I went to bed at 5 a.m. and got up at 8 a.m. on a bright, sunny morning. I fetched wood and coal then went out with the FSO (Field Security Officer), Butch, Tony and Military Police on a search which resulted in the capture of three SS men and another store of arms.

As we crossed the Weser again, this time at Nienburg by Jordan Bridge, I thought, 'Only one more river to cross: the Elbe.' On the way back to camp we met a number of interesting people who had been uprooted by the war and were trying to pick up the threads of a more settled life again: some liberated French and Belgian prisoners of war, an old woman evacuee from Breslau, a Yugoslav officer who was with a Russian girl in a stolen Nazi car, an American soldier wearing British battledress who was an ex-prisoner of war, captured in Normandy. We gave this man a lift as far as Hannover where we handed him over to Field Security.

In Hannover, in addition to the widespread destruction of the physical environment, we came across telling evidence of the breaking up of families and other human relationships when we found hundreds of postcards pinned to shop-fronts, asking for the whereabouts of relatives and other loved ones. These signs of social dislocation were to be seen in all the towns we passed through in north Germany. This journey gave me my first experience of the Reichsautobahn, a foretaste of the motorways that were to come but originally part of Hitler's dream of rapid military conquest. The glorious spring day ended in a violent thunderstorm. All the colours of the landscape were more vivid after the rain, the grass was greener, roofs were redder. Impressive, angry mountains of blue cloud were left in the sky as the storm retreated.

Just as I was going to bed the South African Staff Sergeant van Coller and two others, Sergeant Jones and John Nicholson, arrived with a bottle of wine and the idea of having supper. We had fried eggs on toast (the eggs given to us by the wife of a German farmer imprisoned for nine months for making disparaging remarks about the Nazi regime), with coffee, then drank wine and discussed, among other things, the future of the world, Christianity and the survival of army comradeship. The party broke up at 2.45 a.m.

And so, as the war moved inexorably towards the final chapter of the Germans' defeat, we made faster progress and on our way received more accounts of the shattered morale of the German army.

We were now not far from Belsen and Captain Thornton received an invitation to take a party of us to see a concentration camp for ourselves. At the last minute he declined the offer, perhaps because of a sensitive disposition, or perhaps having already had his fill of horror he did not want to see more. But he was not to be spared. We were to meet some of the camp victims who had spilled on to the road, too weak to walk far, but able to stand by the roadside or lean against a wall to stare at us as we passed. At Fallingbostel we met three living skeletons: two Australian ex-prisoners of war who with an American were trying to get back to England. They had spent part of their captivity in Stalag XIB, and as a result had been reduced to this emaciated state. They had been so hungry in the camp that, though they were friends, they used to fight each other savagely over swede peelings from the dustbins – how little I knew of the reality of starvation. Each day as they were marched away from the battle-front they heard the British artillery following them and expected that at any moment they would be liberated; but they did not wait for this to happen. It was while the Germans, in full retreat, were marching their prisoners back to their own reorganised positions, that these three men dodged the column and stole a car. They told us they had seen fifteen-year-old SS officers and Hitler Youth shooting their own soldiers who refused to fight. During their escape German farmers, terrified by rumours of Allied reprisals, offered to billet them so as to be better treated by the advancing British. We gave the three men a lift for part of their way, fearing that our vehicle would shake them apart.

En route we inspected a trainload of fifteen V2 rockets which had been shelled – filled less for London.

The work of counter-intelligence did not slacken, though we were aware that the end of the war was near. The sudden, surprise reversals of the Ardennes offensive on the one hand and Hitler's constant threats of a secret weapon on the other left no room for complacency in what continued to be a fierce struggle, with the German nation committed by its fanatical leader to a fight to extinction. We had to be on the alert for movements, plots and ambushes which would endanger the life and operations of Tac HQ and its commander. Individuals and groups alike were subject to scrutiny. Attitudes of suspicion and mistrust had, after years of security work, become not only professional requirements but a way of life (to be unlearnt and reversed in later years of peace). I was never very much at ease in this belligerent role, especially when confronted by war-weary, apathetic civilians who, in their anxiety to resume a normal life, offered what help they could to the Allies. At Nienburg we interviewed two men who had suffered badly under the Nazis and gave us names of desperate fanatics likely to cause trouble. So convinced were these German defectors of Allied victory that they no longer feared reprisals from their former tormentors. It was in situations like this that our habitual distrust of denunciators led us to suspect mixed motives. All the time in Germany we were plagued by the question: 'Are these people prompted by a real attraction to the cause of democracy (as understood and advertised by the Allies), or are they activated by a conditioned reflex to submit to the visible uniform-wearing authority currently in power?' Did we insult their intelligence by supposing that the same attitude to all-powerful authority had mesmerised them into obedience to the winning side, or were they simply bowing to the inevitable? Yet there was no obligation on the part of Germans to collaborate with us, and our informers professed to have suffered under the Nazis. On our first arrival in a town or village it was difficult to get hold of the facts, and our attitude to deserters, defectors and denunciators was invariably guarded.

14

TAC IN DANGER

On 20 April Tac was on the move again with all speed: we got up at 6.30 a.m., packed our bedding and kit, and after breakfast loaded the jeep. We left shortly after the advance party which we eventually met up with. The dusty days were back again, reminiscent of Normandy. We crossed the Weser at Hoya and the Aller at Rethen. One of our lorries ran over a dog but such was the urgency of our advance that we could not stop; the long convoy of military vehicles moved on relentlessly. War is full of minor tragedies contained within the major ones.

With the headquarters destined for a life under canvas now that spring had come, our Counter-Intelligence Detachment felt unusually privileged, thanks to the efforts and influence of our commanding officer, Captain Thornton, to enjoy (for want of a better word) our next brief sojourn in the relative comfort of a deserted farmhouse, dismal and dark though it was, in a densely wooded area at least a mile outside the camp. In our search of the creepy building we found a large collection of sporting rifles, ammunition and hunting knives.

Our period of respite did not last long, as we received a warning of a forest fire which was spreading rapidly. This was the first of several such warnings during the course of that night. Houses on the outskirts of the nearby town of Soltau were still smouldering from the recent air raid which must also have caused the forest fire. During our investigation of the fire and its unlikely threat to the main body of the camp, we again encountered the all-too-frequent problem of German deserters and would-be prisoners of war. Instead of going quietly home as so many had been ordered to do by hard-pressed front-line units, they persisted in giving themselves up. Could this have been inspired by the thought of Allied rations and the associated lightening of a burden on their starving families? To us who had to cope with these increasing numbers in addition to our official duties it began to seem as though barbed wire had a strange attraction for German soldiers, disoriented by their unaccustomed freedom from military discipline and the loss of the feeling of security which years of barrack servitude and camp life had given them.

Two soldiers of the Wehrmacht dressed in civilian clothes doggedly waited for three hours to report to us with the same determination with which Londoners were queueing to see *Gone With The Wind*. During the night a young member of the Luftwaffe in uniform came to tell us that he had been on leave to see his child who had died. The Allies had swept past his village during that time and now he was ready to give himself up. He had an open wound in his leg and was wearing a soft slipper on one foot. We told him to spend that night at home and we would call for him in the morning. The next day, 21 April, we went to the house where his wife was living as an evacuee from Hamburg; he was ready, gave his wife a parting kiss and, still wearing his slipper, climbed in the pouring rain into our jeep. After a ten-mile journey, during the course of which he showed his eagerness to condemn the war and discuss the merits of democracy, we left him at the POW Cage, a bleak, rain-soaked field where hundreds of his compatriots in and out of uniform were standing in various attitudes of dejection. We watched him limp through the opening in the barbed wire and become one with that dejected, humiliated crowd.

Tac HQ, which at its inception had looked like a cosy, well-organised gypsy encampment, with its neat rows of tents and caravans, had within the space of a year swollen to the size of a village. Each branch had its line or semicircle of canvas dwellings branching off from the main camp highway. There were clusters of signboards at each road or track junction, the sky was enmeshed in a pattern of wireless aerials and signal wires, and the primeval German woods echoed to the low hum of generators. Within the perimeter lived a busy, friendly, cheerful community.

This time the CI Detachment were outside the homely confines of Tac. Where the last outpost of signal lines dwindled into one or two solitary trucks, followed by an area of dense scrub, far away from the discreet, twinkling lights, the tents and caravans, our ghostly mansion reared itself among the pines. We were well forward this time, and knew that the area had not been entirely cleared of the enemy. We had received a report that three SS battalions were in the district only a few kilometres away, forming a pocket of resistance. I got up at 11.30 p.m. and did my nocturnal tour of guard duty in a howling wind. It was a night of storms and ominous noises, exaggerated no doubt by my own state of nervous apprehension at the nearness of the enemy. Before my next spell of guard duty at 5.30 a.m. I went out in the heavy rain to fetch wood and in the dawn light saw two German armoured cars pass by on the road. A moment later I heard one burst of gunfire, then there was silence.

The next night in that house imposed a greater strain on the nerves, especially as Ken and I were left in sole charge to guard it in the absence of the others who were on various duties following up visits we had made to Military Government and the bürgermeister of Soltau. Left alone, Ken and I stoked the fire, lit a lamp and candles, and secured the black-out. The noise of gunfire became more persistent and seemed to be coming nearer. We sat still and listened, scarcely daring to breathe. Then the silence was broken by the telephone ringing in the next room. The call was from the Officer Commanding the Defence Company, Major Weaver, telling us in an urgent voice:

'The pocket, four thousand men strong and two miles away, is advancing towards your house. I strongly advise you to get out.'

We had barely recovered from the impact of that message when the telephone rang again. This time it was Major Odgers saying crisply:

'We are expecting some visitors tonight, and I recommend you to evacuate yourselves into the camp area. How many of you are there? I see. Well, please yourselves. If you decide to stay, barricade yourselves in and at the first signs of attack open fire with everything you've got. Anyway, make a hell of a noise, and Defence Company will come to your rescue.'

Then there was silence except for the insistent whine of the wind in the surrounding trees. Ken and I both expressed our sudden longing for the protection afforded by the distant line of tents. If only the others would come: we couldn't leave without them. How could we warn them when we didn't know where they were? We started to do the only thing possible in the circumstances, and that was to set about barricading ourselves in and destroying documents that would betray the nearby location of Tac HQ. Why didn't the rest of the detachment come? Fear found a natural outlet in anger: 'Isn't it just typical to be away at a time like this.'

Then we both turned and looked at each other. What was that? Someone was at the door. It started with a mouselike scratching and gradually developed into a persistent rattling of the door handle. We rose as one, neither of us wishing to play the coward, yet neither of us in a very great hurry to get to the door. Then someone began putting all his weight against our partially-constructed barricade.

A voice said: 'What the hell's going on?' It was Len, our driver.

There was no time to explain before the jeep arrived with Captain Thornton, Tony and Butch. All soon realised the gravity of the situation. The house was in the direct path of the approaching Panzers, the rumble of whose tanks could now be heard. There followed a feverish loading of our vehicles and the final destruction of our papers and we were off. Never was a move accomplished with such speed. There were no last minute searches for lost articles and none of the usual arguments about where to put what.

We arrived at Tac to find the whole camp on full alert, all personnel at battle stations, even cooks and clerks wearing complete battle order and the sentries and Defence Company ready for the order to fire. We spent much of that night listening to the distant rumbling of tanks and the unmistakable rattle of their tracks – that was all. By some miracle they passed us by, unaware that the headquarters of our C-in-C, one of the most vital nerve centres of Allied war effort, was so close.

The next morning we breathed again, but on returning to the house in the woods we could verify from the evidence of tank tracks and broken trees that the enemy had indeed passed that way. They were annihilated by a brigade of 53 Div; we had been lucky. However, our 'visitors' had claimed one victim: Major John Poston, one of Tac's most vivid liaison officers and a former ADC to General Montgomery, was killed when he ran into a Nazi ambush on his return to camp from a news-gathering mission to the front line. Machine gunners opened fire when they saw him approach, but he drove his jeep hard at them and we were informed that he did not die alone. On Wednesday 25 April, Tactical Headquarters assembled in a field for Major Poston's funeral. He was buried with full military honours on the edge of the forest.

The 26 April was the first anniversary of the formation of Tac HQ. Since that day one year ago Tac had moved twenty-seven times and travelled over eleven hundred miles from the Normandy beaches.

On 1 May 1945 I got up at 6.30 a.m., packed my kit and searched the camp area with the Defence Company rear party for our last war-time move to Lüneburg Heath. I reported our move to the Military Government and delivered the necessary information to local field security sections. On our journey we saw vast damage and wrecked locomotives in bombed marshalling yards. We watched 'ack-ack' tracers pursuing planes as they circled overhead, and as daylight was fading we saw flares in the sky over the River Elbe.

On Lüneburg Heath we were given new tents. At 10.30 p.m. while I was in bed an announcement was made over the German radio that Adolf Hitler had fallen in battle that afternoon.

15

SURRENDER

3 May 1945

T he CI Detachment were called upon to mount a
twenty-four-hour guard over some German visitors
who had arrived to see the Commander-in-Chief. They
were soon to become famous throughout the world. They
and Lüneburg Heath were, in a few hours' time, destined for
the history books.

4 May 1945

In the afternoon there was conspicuous activity in the
neighbourhood of a marquee which had been newly erected
in front of the C-in-C's mess. At approximately 4 p.m. the
Chief himself came out of his caravan and, crossing over to
the marquee, which was open on one side, seated himself at
the table as if to get the feel of it. He looked all round him
and, beaming with obvious satisfaction at what he saw,
returned to his caravan. At 6 p.m. there was a buzz of
excitement followed by a general move of officers towards
the main camp entrance. A few minutes later they returned
and three German staff cars rolled into the visitors' car
park, bearing with them:

General-Admiral von Friedeburg, C-in-C of the German
  Navy, successor to Admiral Doenitz
General Kinzel, Chief of Staff to Field Marshal Busch
Rear-Admiral Wagner, staff officer to Admiral von
  Friedeburg
Major Friedel, staff officer to General Kinzel

They were then joined by another staff officer, Colonel Pollek, and the whole delegation was paraded under the Union Jack on Monty's caravan site. Admiral von Friedeburg was taken by the Chief into his caravan and after a short while came out and rejoined the other members of his party. It was at this moment that about forty war correspondents bore down upon the C-in-C's area. One of them with an injured foot was being carried by two others. The look of determination on his face seemed to indicate that even if his foot had dropped off he still intended to reach that open marquee. Tony and I had by this time taken up our stand with the CMP at the opening of the marquee. The five German figureheads made an impressive picture as they moved from the Visitors' Camp towards the crowd assembled below. There was no red carpet for them. They strode through the heather and, emerging through the last graceful cluster of silver birches by the Field Marshal's caravan, halted just inside the entrance to the marquee. A minute or two elapsed and the Commander-in-Chief, in his smart be-ribboned battledress and famous beret, walked briskly past the throng of Press representatives. He smiled at them then turned to face the Germans, who saluted smartly and waited until he was seated before sitting down themselves. There were microphones on the simple trestle table, which was covered with an army blanket, and a barrage of cameras was trained from all sides on the small group sitting there. The voice of Field Marshal Montgomery was clear and crisp as he read the surrender terms. The Germans sat with mask-like faces as they listened to the words which sealed the fate of their land, sea and air forces in Holland and northwest Germany, including all islands, and Denmark. Tony and I could hardly conceal our excitement at being witnesses to this great historical proceeding. We stood out among that distinguished company of top brass, for with the Corps of Military Police we were the only other ranks present, a fact noticed by Rex North of the *Sunday Pictorial*, who took down our names and particulars of our army service. After each of the Germans had signed in turn, Field Marshal Montgomery said:

'Now I will sign on behalf of the Supreme Commander, General Eisenhower.'

The tent flaps were then lowered and Monty was alone with the chiefs whose forces he had pursued in campaigns that had taken him from El Alamein and on to Lübeck.

Of the four German plenipotentiaries who came to see the Chief on 3 May, only Rear-Admiral Wagner survived to take his part in the West German administration. The other three died in tragic circumstances very soon after the surrender. General-Admiral von Friedeburg took poison, General Kinzel shot himself and Major Friedel died in a car accident on 21 May; Tony, who was acting as his escort, escaped with a minor injury.

6 May 1945

On the evening of 6 May I was summoned to the Colonel GSI's caravan and told to be ready to leave early the next morning for an important assignment. I was given no details except that I should be introduced to Major O'Brien, one of Field Marshal Montgomery's Liaison Officers, who would explain what was required of me.

7 May 1945

It was a sparkling spring day, but apart from the bright May sunshine this unforgettable day started as so many other days of Army life – with a host of unexciting chores. After tidying my bed space in the tent, taking two pairs of boots to the cobbler, giving the daily strength return to the Camp Sergeant Major and packing my small kit, I reported for duty soon after dawn at the given map reference on Lüneburg Heath.

Punctually at the appointed time I was met by two British officers in a jeep. One of them was Major O'Brien and the other turned out to be an observer from the BBC, Chester Wilmot. Giving them my smartest salute I climbed into the jeep. We were driven across the bumpy heath and through the outskirts of the town of Lüneburg to the airfield where an Anson was already waiting for us as we pulled up. Excitement took complete possession of me as I boarded the plane on this, my very first flight – air travel had not yet become the everyday experience it is now. We were strapped into our seats, the small iron ladder was drawn up into the plane, the door was shut, and with a roar of engines we slid along the runway towards that warm blue sky. Soon Germany lay neat and geometrical far below us. Where were the dust and the potholes, the wreckage of the marshalling yards, the endless, untidy, heartbreaking processions of displaced persons in that now over-simplified landscape? I gazed down upon the sunlit Elbe, gliding in a sinuous ribbon through a bright patchwork of green and yellow fields; in the distance rose the few remaining chimneys of Hamburg. Later the Kiel Canal cut a straight line across the view. Now and again the plane bumped up or dropped down as it hit an air pocket. I looked at Major O'Brien for some hint of information about the object of our journey. Drawing from his pocket a large envelope he said to me:

'This, my boy, is the end of the war.'

I had witnessed the signing of the cease-fire terms presided over by Field Marshal Montgomery on 4 May, but the Germans were still fighting against the Russians and in other theatres of war: for them the war continued. This day was to signal the end of all hostilities in the west. I was elated at the prospect of final surrender, which would at last bring peace throughout Europe; I felt like singing.

But what was a mere sergeant doing on this vital mission? Major O'Brien caught my look of enquiry:

'You speak German don't you Sergeant?'

'Yes Sir.'

'Well then.'

I thought, 'What is that supposed to mean?' and imagined

having to play the usual boring part of standing guard or telling my two superior officers where the cloakrooms were. I could not have been more mistaken. Major O'Brien had been entrusted with the task of delivering a letter containing the final surrender terms into the hands of Field Marshal Keitel, Supreme Head of the German Armed Forces, and I was to be the interpreter. The BBC reporter was to be introduced as an army captain, assistant to the major.

A large German aerodrome hove in sight with planes bearing the swastika standing in neat rows round the edges of the field. These, we learned, were all that remained of Goering's mighty Luftwaffe. I remembered having seen other planes with those same markings littering the fields of Kent. I had memories too of the planes which kept Londoners awake during the long nights of the Blitz. The Anson veered over and twice circled the airfield before landing. Owing to some misunderstanding there was no one to meet the delegates from Field Marshal Montgomery's Tactical Headquarters, but a German general, General Blaskowitz, who happened to be on the spot, came towards us and announced:

'I know of no such mission.'

He did, however, volunteer to drive the party to OKW (*Oberkommando der Wehrmacht*, the Supreme Headquarters of the German Armed Forces) in his car.

In the streets of Flensburg, crowded with German soldiers, sailors, airmen and civilians, the three British uniforms in the open-top car caused a great stir. The soldiers in that mass of people were a remnant of the retreating armies that had escaped capture on the Russian Front. They looked demoralised and abandoned, gaunt and grey-faced; many were unshaven and unshod, with bare feet poking through strips of rag. Some wore long tattered coats and dirty, frayed trousers – a scene reminiscent of the retreat from Moscow. Arms raised stiffly in Nazi salutes greeted the general all along the road, but the events of that day would bring about the end of such demonstrations. Major O'Brien whispered:

'Don't get big ideas, Sergeant – they're not saluting you. It's the swastika on the bonnet.'

From that day it would be a punishable offence to raise the arm in a '*Sieg Heil*' salute or to display the Nazi flag in public.

The German Supreme Headquarters was located in a Naval School where steel-helmeted sentries guarded the entrances and patrolled the grounds, a duty which, in a matter of minutes, was to lose its point. As we stepped out of the car there was a general clicking of heels, like hundreds of castanets, and a flutter of Nazi salutes. Chester Wilmot and I both caught a glimpse of Field Marshal Keitel standing at an upstairs bay window, before we were ushered into the building. A long passage lay before us. More helmeted sentries with rifles slung and hand-grenades wedged in their belts were giving more Nazi salutes outside office doors. Two civilian visitors were having their identity checked in the all-too-familiar way. At the end of the corridor our party was shown into a small barely furnished room crammed with German officers. As we entered we were asked to sit down and one of them rose to his feet and took up his position, legs astride, with his back to the door. We were asked to explain the purpose of our visit.

'Tell them,' said Major O'Brien to me.

In quivering German, but struggling to steady my voice, I explained that the major and the captain his assistant had come from Field Marshal Montgomery's Headquarters with a copy of the final terms of surrender. Major O'Brien carried the document and demanded to place it in the hands of Field Marshal Keitel. They appeared not to believe us. Major Buchs who was the spokesman for the Germans said in a quiet, measured voice:

'This message comes as a surprise.'

It was then that I noticed, through the high window opposite to where I was sitting, the tip of a bayonet passing at intervals backwards and forwards. They had placed a guard on the room. We were kept waiting what seemed a very long time and Major O'Brien's impatience with this treatment had to be translated into firmer German. I shall always remember that dingy room, where a solemn picture of Adolf Hitler was jostled by lighter works of art including a humorous study of some little boys fishing.

Major Buchs objected that we could not see Field Marshal Keitel as he had just gone out. This news came as a shock to us; the urgent message required the instant delivery by hand of the surrender terms and had we not just seen Field Marshal Keitel? There was something not quite straightforward about this reception. We protested: did they not realise the importance of our mission? I repeated:

'We insist that we have come from Field Marshal Montgomery's Headquarters with the requested copy of the final terms of surrender.'

At this moment the proceedings were interrupted by a sharp rap on the door. A German orderly, bowing stiffly from the waist, announced *Mittagessen*.

'It is time for lunch,' declared Major Buchs, shelving any further decision.

Major O'Brien held firm:

'My instructions from General Eisenhower are to place this letter in the hands of Field Marshal Keitel.'

'But that is impossible if he is not here,' replied the major.

There was nothing to be done about that and presumably the business of checking our credentials was proceeding somewhere in the background. All sorts of unpleasant thoughts were beginning to stir in my mind and I could sense that my companions shared my uneasiness. While we were waiting in the room we heard gangs of soldiers return from their morning's work singing staccato marching songs. Then came a ray of hope in the form of a telephone message from Tac with instructions to collect Seyss-Inquart, the infamous Gauleiter (Provincial Governor) of Holland, and bring him back in the same plane with us.

Shortly after this two staff cars (the only Mercedes Benzes left in Germany, according to Major Buchs) drew up outside the main entrance and we were invited to travel in them to lunch. Major O'Brien and Chester Wilmot took their seats in the rear car while I sat in British isolation in the leading car. Beside the driver sat the German major and, standing stiffly next to me in the back of the open Mercedes, a German guard with steel helmet concealing all of his face but his lower jaw, waved traffic to one side with a white baton. This white stick with a red disc at one end of it gave us priority. Nazi salutes and clicking heels greeted our passage through the town as, with siren screaming, we swept into the approach to the German Officers' Mess down by the water's edge. It was here that I saw Denmark for the first time. Unfortunately this last country to be liberated by the armies of the West was across the water, inaccessible yet to tantalisingly near.

On arrival at the officers' mess I felt very lonely as I waited for the other car containing my only two allies in a hostile Germany. Looking across the lake I thought, 'After they've shot us I suppose that is where they'll dump the bodies.' I was shaken out of this dispiriting reverie when, to my relief, Major O'Brien and Chester Wilmot came at last and went into the Mess. I waited outside. A few moments later Major O'Brien reappeared and said:

'Come on in, Sergeant.'

'I can't, Sir,' I answered.

'Why not?'

'I'm only a sergeant.'

'Well, they're only Nazis.'

So I went in, to be confronted by an assembly of German officers of all ranks, from the lowest to the highest.

The lunch in the Officers' Mess, where the waiters seemed petrified whenever an order was given, consisted of thick barley soup resembling dirty rice pudding, one slice of black bread and a glass of wine. The latter was excellent and proved to be the one redeeming feature of the meal. With ambiguous modesty my German neighbour at the table (a brigadier) apologised:

'You see to what Germany has been reduced when the

leaders of the people have to eat such filth. But never mind. We did save this good wine with which to celebrate *our* victory. Ha! Ha!'

This sarcastic reference to their defeat was surprising on the lips of a high-ranking German officer before the publication of the surrender terms.

When the meal was over an orderly burst into the room and, jumping to attention with clicking heels, breathlessly delivered his message to the senior officer present:

'Field Marshal Keitel awaits the British representatives.'

We again climbed into the staff cars and drove back to Field Marshal Keitel's office in the OKW. This proved to be an unpretentious room overlooking the main entrance from where we had caught our first glimpse of Keitel. Clerks were bustling about in what appeared to be an undisciplined and undignified muddle in the small anteroom from which we were ushered into the presence of Keitel himself. We had to edge our way between an obtruding filing cabinet and a dishevelled girl typist who, with hair falling over her machine, was tapping out a training programme for the Germany Army for the year 1947. Training for what? The next war? And what German Army?

As the narrow door leading into Keitel's room swung open I was still wrestling mentally with the ordeal of having to translate military jargon into German. Suppose he rejected the terms! That would be awkward. All sorts of embarrassing possibilities suggested themselves, but it was too late. We were already over the threshold and the august figures of Keitel and his Chief of Staff stood silhouetted against the window. That is how I shall always remember them. There was a tense moment of deathly silence. Of course! They were waiting for the interpreter to speak first! We walked up to the field marshal's desk and, with a brisk salute, I took the plunge by introducing Major O'Brien the Liaison Officer, and the captain, his assistant, and was struck by the weighty climax to which my words built up when spoken in the German order:

'Herr Feld Marschall may I present to you Major O'Brien who, from Field Marshal Montgomery's Headquarters, on behalf of General Eisenhower, Supreme Commander of the Allied Forces in Europe, has brought the final terms of surrender of German Armed Forces on land, on sea and in the air.'

I was even more amazed to think that it was my voice which had actually made this solemn announcement of the war's end to the Supreme Head of the German Wehrmacht. Field Marshal Keitel, an imposing figure in those drab surroundings, opened the letter which the LO presented to him and with a face like granite replied:

'Thank you for this document containing the text of the surrender terms. I am already acquainted with those terms through General Jodl, who has communicated with me from General Eisenhower's Headquarters, whither I despatched him this morning, but I require and will keep this letter as security.'

When people speak English or French you know what they are saying while they are saying it. When people are speaking in German you don't know what they are saying until after they have finished. Field Marshal Keitel's reply went something like this:

'I you, for this surrendertermscontaing,requiredassecurity document the message of which has been communicated to me from General Eisenhower's Headquarters by the thitherdespatched General Jodl this morning, thank.'

Waiting desperately for the final verb (suppose it had been 'curse' or 'defy' or 'challenge'?) which was to make sense of what seemed an endless sentence, I turned half-left in military style to the liaison officer and translated the Field Marshal's words by simply saying:

'He said "Thank you".'

Major O'Brien's raised eyebrows seemed to imply, 'Did he really?'

In conclusion Keitel said:

'And thank Field Marshal Montgomery for the promptitude with which he has sent you.'

He grasped his baton and gave a smart salute by holding it obliquely across his chest. The monocle in his eye wobbled with this sudden movement of his body. We too saluted, in less spectacular fashion, turned right-about and walked out of the room.

Our next duty was to find Seyss-Inquart. He must have been tipped off, because he had made his getaway, and our enquiries only met with negative response. He could not be found. He was, however, picked up later on the road by the Canadian Army, who in order to discourage any further absconding took away his false teeth. It was our suspicion that Admiral Doenitz had also deliberately made himself scarce, leaving Field Marshal Keitel in charge, but he did not get very far either and all were eventually brought to trial at Nürnberg.

In the course of our enquiries we learned a few facts about the last days of Hitler's Headquarters. The German colonel whom we pumped, though he had seen Adolf Hitler himself as late as 20 April, could give no facts about the Führer's death; he had only heard of it over the wireless. Shortly after this, on about 23 April, OKW moved from Berlin to Flensburg. Their convoy was not attacked during this move, which took place both in daylight and at night. The colonel had watched Allied planes attack another convoy acting as a decoy, but theirs arrived unscathed. We asked if Himmler were at Flensburg. He said, 'Perhaps.' He volunteered the already stale information that Goering had been taken prisoner by the Americans in the south, and that Goebbels as well as Hitler had died.

In the middle of our rather one-sided conversation, which had resolved itself into a political quiz, the German liaison officer returned with the dubious information that unfortunately Seyss-Inquart had left for Field Marshal Montgomery's Headquarters by car.

As our small party of three emerged from OKW, walked down the front steps and climbed into the Mercedes Benz which was to take us to the airfield, German officers lined up with their cameras and took photographs.

Only when the Anson roared up towards the blue again did I sink back in delicious relaxation.

8 May 1945

VE-Day and the end of the war in Europe.

German Guests at Tac HQ

My day began on 8 May by my having to meet and escort a convoy of German staff cars on their journey to Tac HQ. The German officers, with their staff, were to reside at Tac on a site adjacent to ours, the only demarcation line being a length of tape. I was to move in with the Germans and from now on, with the war over and Field Marshal Montgomery cast in the role of administrator rather than subjugator of Germany, my work was increasingly that of an interpreter. This job started immediately with linguistic duties in the Visitors' camp, then going with a German lieutenant and his cook in a German staff car, followed by a 15 cwt truck, to the office of the Oberbürgermeister of Lüneburg to requisition beds, mattresses and kitchen utensils for the German camp. (We had come a long way from the time when, in Normandy, the headquarters went into a state of alarm at the discovery of one terrified German teenage soldier caught hiding inside our camp; now, on the very first day of peace, a whole array of German top brass had arrived to move in with our Commander-in-Chief. It could not have happened yesterday, and would have been beyond belief at any earlier stage.)

In these incredible circumstances I listened to Mr Churchill's victory speech on the radio with my new German associates, who were quietly attentive, and at 9 p.m. in the Sergeants' Mess I listened to the King's speech.

After supper a message came from the British camp next door (that is from Tac HQ) requiring my immediate presence at G(Ops). The G2 said,

160

'Good evening, Sergeant Kirby. You have been released from your escort duties for a day to do a special job tomorrow. I want you to go to this map reference and find out all you can about a certain countess. She is an English woman married to a German. Clear?'

'Not completely, Sir. Do I receive an introduction to her?'

'No.'

'What kind of information do you want?'

'Anything you can get.'

'From a security angle?'

'No particular angle.'

'Is she a war criminal?'

'No!'

'Can I say who sent me?'

'No.'

'Rather vague isn't it, Sir?'

'Yes, but that's all we can tell you.'

At that moment the telephone rang and the G2 became involved in a long, slightly technical conversation.

'All right, Sergeant? Leave whenever you like tomorrow morning,' he whispered, by way of saying goodbye.

There was something exhilarating about the mystery which surrounded this job, and I went to bed that night in a mood of expectancy, mingled with the excitement and relief shared by all of us that the war was over. This excitement materialised in the shape of a gigantic bonfire lit by the ORs in the camp in response to the many distant fires which had been started by other army units stationed in different parts of Lüneburg Heath and to the joyful red, green, yellow and white flares which lit up the sky and country for miles around. One of our men carrying a jerrycan had climbed a tall pine tree and on reaching the top poured out its contents so that the whole tree was soaked in petrol. When he was safely on the ground someone threw on a lighted match and we had a bonfire to end all bonfires. We then joined hands and danced round the blaze, singing lustily in carefree abandon.

These high spirits were brought to an abrupt end by the sudden appearance of the G2(Ops) ordering us to extinguish the fire at once. This unpopular command was prompted partly, we thought, by fears for the safety of the camp, but on further reflection, perhaps also by the idea that our euphoria was prematurely expressed, as hostilities were officially to cease only at one minute after midnight. (Yes, but then what about this German Headquarters living with us?) It would no doubt have been unseemly for Field Marshal Montgomery's Headquarters to have been seen to jump the gun. The order was obeyed with much murmuring.

The next morning, 9 May, before setting out on my day's mission I attended a conference of Intelligence staff with Colonel Ewart, concerning the administration of the German camp.

It was not until 11.20 a.m. that I was free to draw rations and make ready for my journey. I then found that there was no transport available. One of our jeeps had come to rest in the REME workshops at the close of its hectic career, and Tony was out with the remaining one. There was nothing left for it but to apply to the MT office for a car – after all a car would probably have a more potent influence over a countess than a jeep. Negotiations at the MT office proved highly successful: I managed to obtain not only a car but a driver as well. With a Cipher sergeant to keep me company I set off in style to find the countess. This was the day on which Europe, after five and a half years of war, was drawing its first breaths of peace and freedom. It was spring and we were in high spirits as we drove through the fresh green countryside under a bright May sky. Much of the journey was spent in speculating how we were to obtain an introduction to the countess, and be plausible after having done so. All sorts of suggestions were put forward: first of all we would have a puncture and call at the Schloss for a bowl of water. That would not do because the countess would not, in the first place, open the door herself; in the second place, she would not carry water for three ORs. Then there was the idea that we could be representatives from Psychological Warfare trying to build up a picture of German civilian reactions to our occupation. There were snags in this too, as none of us was very sure about what Psychological Warfare did. We were beginning to realise that rank had its privileges even in the ordinary details of life. We could not say that we had met one of the lady's relatives, because we would soon be out of our depth. Then, like a bolt out of the blue, came the winning suggestion. We would go as members of the Red Cross who were trying to make contact with British-born civilians in Germany, for reasons of welfare and morale at home. Our first task was to remove our cap badges, after which we must try to secure a couple of Red Cross armbands. By this time we were approaching our destination and soon we caught sight of an imposing façade above some trees round a bend in the road. This was the Schloss. We had to think quickly. On a closer inspection of the place our hopes faded. British army lorries were lined up in the garden and courtyard, tents were pitched under the trees and the smoke of an army cookhouse rose from the stables. Everywhere we looked we found the army in complete possession. We would never find the countess here. Nevertheless the necessary enquiries must be made. At the Signals Office I was pleased to learn that the countess was in residence. The Intelligence Officer was most helpful and produced a file containing her history. The Schloss belonged to another countess with whom our countess was living as an evacuee. Both were English women married to Germans. Their husbands were officers in the German army. The husband of the one in whom we were interested was a prisoner in Italy.

As it was lunchtime we decided to eat our sandwiches in the car first and have our interview afterwards. Half an hour later, fortified by spam and jam, armed with an adequate history of the countess and inspired by our own brilliant subterfuge, we introduced ourselves to the officer who was to open the necessary doors for us. This is only a figure of speech, for no doors opened into the countess' apartments. With the exception of two rooms reserved for her, the château was completely militarised. Rooms which might have been the count's library or his wife's boudoir now bore such prosaic labels as Signal Office, MI Room, or Officers' Mess. The two women were not allowed to use either the front or the back door. Their only entrance was by means of a ladder propped up against their window. The officer told us to wait for the countess in the garden: her friend had gone to fetch her.

We had a pleasant surprise in store for us. After preparing ourselves mentally for some formidable presence of indeterminate age, we were taken aback when a beautiful woman in her middle or late twenties suddenly appeared behind a high bank of tulips. She greeted us simply and warmly with a frank, unaffected smile. Her fair hair was loose and fell slightly over one eye; she kept tossing it back as the wind caught it. Her feet were bare, with red painted toenails. She believed our Red Cross story (even without any arm bands) and said happily:

'At last I shall be able to get in touch with Mother.'

She was therefore more than willing to communicate, her gratitude making us feel caddish. While we were talking to her and her friend, an officer came up to us to ask us what we wanted. It was a tense moment. We edged him away to one side and explained our mission. He said he was a cousin of the lady who owned the Schloss, which spoiled our philanthropic pose, as here they had on their own doorstep a relative who could give them all the home news they wanted. The situation became less awkward when the officer very decently suggested going for a walk with his cousin, to leave us alone with the countess. As the other two left us the countess said:

'Let us go into the house. Please excuse our ladder.'

She climbed up in her bare feet and we followed. The room we found ourselves in was quiet, spacious, comfortably furnished and full of spring flowers. Sunlight streamed through the long windows and delicate shadows of leaves and branches flickered over the white walls. An arrangement of tulips formed a colourful background against the countess' head as she sat on a low divan, with her bare feet sunk into the thick pile of the white carpet.

This contact with an English mind, closed for six years from the current of public opinion in England, proved to be interesting and full of surprises. Some of the countess' views were fascinating, others were deeply shocking. The war had passed over her without a ripple. She confessed that she could not have come through the war more comfortably, and the Germans had all been so kind and charming to her. She expressed blank amazement at the concept of anyone hating the Germans at all. To her they were friendly, placid, child-like people, incapable of hatred. They never had any heart for the war, and the people of north-west Germany in particular had no love for the Nazis. They looked upon the Tommies as liberators and only wanted to be friends with the British. I commented that the Allies had been looked upon as liberators in France too, to which she replied:

'These Latin races welcome any foreign troops for the sheer novelty of it. The Germans were welcomed when they first went to France. They behaved themselves correctly and were highly admired. Then you came, and it made a change for them, so you were welcomed.'

She went on to say that the Germans had such a good opinion of the British that it was a pity the first soldiers to arrive in the village should have done so much looting. Now that was being regulated and the people were more at ease again. When the British troops first arrived in the village she was very anxious lest they might shoot the Kreis Kommandmant:

'It would have been too terrible! He is such a charming man, and he has been so very good to us. When I was called up to do war work in one of those awful ammunition factories, the Kommandant got me out of it. Instead I have to work for a few hours in the garden each day.'

She expressed more sorrow over the plight of Germans in the Russian zone of occupation than for the victims of Nazi oppression. She sincerely believed that the Russians murdered every house-holder in Germany and deported the children to Siberia. For her the Poles too were a wild, undisciplined people who plundered wherever they went. In her disgust at their lawless behaviour there was no attempt to seek a reason for it. She seemed not to have heard of conditions in Nazi-occupied Europe.

The countess then asked:

'When are we going to get something to eat? It's ages since we had any tea or coffee.'

In answer to this I could not refrain from speaking of Holland on the verge of starvation and of the need to feed our Allies. Almost as an afterthought:

'People at home must eat too.' I said.

'Of course,' the countess agreed.

She then asked if the British authorities treated the German prisoners well. We reassured her.

'The British prisoners of war have been very well looked after here, you know,' she said, and added that on their release the prisoners distributed gifts to the German villagers who had been so kind to them.

The recent reports of conditions in the newly liberated concentration camps were very much on our minds, and when the conversation turned to prisoners and camps I asked the countess if she had heard of Belsen or Buchenwald. She admitted that not until we came did any of the German civilians know of the horrors of those places. They had heard of Dachau which they knew to be rather stricter than other camps. There were, however, rumours among Germans that the heaps of dead bodies found in the camps had been victims of Allied bombing raids. Talk of bombing brought the conversation round to the 1940 Blitz and the nightmare year when our island stood alone against the crushing might of Nazi Germany: the 'Go To It' slogan, the 'Blood, Sweat and Tears' speech of Churchill in Britain's darkest hour, to be followed by the V1 flying bombs and the V2 rockets. The countess listened attentively, then with apparent sincerity said:

'How awful! But then, if the war had lasted six months, as we had all expected it would, everything would have been all right. How were the Germans to know it would last for six years?'

In all her remarks about the war the countess showed how considerably she had been influenced by German propaganda. Who could blame her? Nobody had told her what was at stake. On her own admission she had spent the best years of her life in Germany, and while in her teens had fallen in love and married there. In spite of her opinions and pro-German sympathies she professed unfailing loyalty to England, though she was worried about the reception she might have on her return to that country.

After an hour of fascinating conversation we had satisfied ourselves about many aspects of the countess' circumstances, her health, her family, her living conditions both during the war and at the present time, her state of mind, her political allegiance and her ambivalent though affectionate attitude to the land of her birth.

At this juncture the other countess returned. She too was smiling and looked a picture of health. We rose to leave and as we said goodbye the countess embarrassed us with expressions of gratitude. She ran lightly, still bare-footed, across the carpet and held the curtain back for our descent down the ladder.

We arrived back at Tac in time for the Sergeants' Mess VE-Day dinner, to which ENSA had been invited. I played the piano for our concert then retired at a late hour to my tent to write my report on the countess for Major Odgers.

He later thanked and congratulated me for the report. The information it contained was said to be 'Just right.'

On the morning of 11 May I had to escort our German visitors to the MO for medical inspection and delousing, a routine procedure for troops who had spent so many months in the field. I returned in time for the group photograph of the sergeants with the C-in-C, then joined Major Odgers, Captain Machin and Mr James in the search for a rest resort for the men of Tac HQ. Travemünde was crowded with wounded and badly mutilated German soldiers and a hotel which we had visited the day before was being used as flats for bombed-out people; evacuees were everywhere. So Lübeck with its beautiful lake, boating and leisure facilities was chosen as the place where the men could spend a weekend leave and recuperate from the stresses of war.

It was a rest day on 12 May but there was a great commotion as another lorry-load of Germans arrived.

Sunday 13 May was very hot and sunny. At 9.30 a.m. I escorted a German general and another German officer on a country walk during which we carried on a polite and stilted conversation: prompted by the scenery, and the plant and animal life on our way. The general admired the views across the heath, the fresh spring colours of the trees and wanted to know the English equivalents of the German names:

'What is *Kaninchen* in English?'

A discussion about different animals and birds led almost inevitably to talk about other denizens of the air. My companions felt free to speak about German and British aircraft, comparing our Austers not unfavourably with the German Storchs.

This being the first Sunday since the end of hostilities, we had a special Church Parade which all attended. After the Thanksgiving Service, which was held in the open in a clump of pines on the heath, where the altar with its wooden cross and two bowls of lilac looked surreal against the tree trunks, Monty gave one of his most informal and humorous addresses. He started by saying:

You will probably think, now that the war in Europe is over, that Tac will cease to function and that you can all go home. That is far from the case. Far from it.

He spoke of the present by saying that now that the eyes of the world were on this historic place, he had asked for the camp to be rearranged and tidied up. Of the future he said:

Now that that the war in Europe is over we have a colossal task before us. A colossal task. Compared with the task of organising the peace, winning the war was easy. To begin with, someone is going to have to govern Germany. Whoever it is will go mad in a very short time. That someone is me. Germany is going to be carved up into four zones: a Russian zone, an American zone, a British zone and a French zone. The French zone will be slightly smaller than the others. Our British zone will be of a considerable size and I have been chosen to govern it. The centre will be somewhere near Hannover, to which place Main will move. They will reign there for a matter of ten years or so. Tac will stay here for about six weeks as this is quite a nice place. I intend to have a good look round for a nice château somewhere, or Schloss as the Germans call it. At the moment I have got my eye on Ostenwalde, and we shall probably move back there.

The war is over, and we are all very thankful this is so; one was really getting quite exhausted by the whole business. Now I have to settle down to the biggest battle of all. Fighting Germans is easy compared with the job of dealing with the politicians, or statesmen as I believe they are called. Mr Winston Churchill can be quite trying at times. Getting what I want from the politicians will not be easy. With a General Election ahead of them they've got their votes to think of.

One of the first problems we have to grapple with is the sifting and disbanding of millions of German soldiers. I have decided to push them up into three peninsulas in the north. They will be pushed up against the sea on three sides and sealed off. Then when we have decided who, amongst this crowd of German prisoners, are the doctors, the architects, the miners, the bricklayers, the grocers,

169

the lawyers, the dockers and so on, we will send them back to work in civilian clothes. In a short time we hope to see uniforms banished completely from the German scene. In this way we intend to stamp out all traces of German militarism. Then comes the great problem of reconstruction. Germans will have to be fed, clothed, housed and given medical attention. All these points I hope to bring up when I go to England tomorrow.

Now about this German camp we have in our midst. In order to organise the movement of the vast hordes of German soldiers in our zone, I can only achieve my objective by help from the German commanders who are now working under me to this end. We have a tremendous number of German soldiers to deal with. I am told that tens of thousands are on their way down from the Baltic. The Russians should have taken them over, but they're on their way here.

The officers in the German camp will act as a liaison between Field Marshal Busch's HQ and Tac. He came here and started belly-aching, and I said, 'That's enough of that!' I told him exactly what I think of him. You've got to put these Germans in their place sometimes. The Canadians kept Seyss-Inquart prisoner by robbing him of his false teeth. That's a new one on me.

In that same confiding and jocular tone Monty ended his talk, then wished us all luck in the job ahead, himself included.

The next day in the German camp I saw Lieutenant-Colonel (recently Major) Friedel, one of the German plenipotentiaries who I was to escort the following morning. I gave him the necessary maps, collected a pass for the journey from G(Ops) and rations from the Mess as we were to make an early start. The pass was to prove a most vital safeguard, as I was going to be travelling in a German staff car with uniformed German officers through British-held territory. At that time there were no German soldiers moving freely on the roads. They were either under guard, in prison, in hospital, or dead.

I then went with the German driver to fill up the Mercedes with petrol. I came back to the tent, shaved, and packed my small kit in readiness for the journey.

At 4 a.m. I got up and saw lights in two of the German tents go on. I waited in the Mercedes while Lieutenant-Colonel Friedel and Captain Tinius, the two German officers to be escorted, had their breakfast. Our destination was General Blaskowitz's headquarters in Hilversum. The thought of going to Holland again was exciting. It would be a relief to escape for a while from the resentful atmosphere of Germany. At 4.30 a.m. in the grey of early morning the Mercedes rolled silently over the bumps of Lüneburg Heath towards the main road. Lieutenant-Colonel Friedel sat next to the German driver and I shared the back seat with Captain Tinius. Along the Hamburg–Bremen Autobahn the car travelled for certain stretches at 120 kph – measured in kilometres the speed looked truly impressive. Bridges carrying other roads flashed by overhead in rapid succession. The special pass from G(Ops) which I was carrying proved to be indispensable at all the towns and bridges. The car was challenged an untold number of times by sentries and policemen, both civil and military. On two breathtaking occasions we nearly came under fire from the Sten guns of enthusiastic guards.

Incredible as it may be to imagine officers and staff of the German High Command taking up residence at Field Marshal Montgomery's Headquarters with effect from VE day, from the moment that hostilities ceased, at least the British residents of Tac HQ had had this extraordinary event explained to them with great clarity by the Commander-in-Chief himself. My position therefore as a lodger in the German camp was understood and accepted with characteristic tolerance and teasing by my friends. However, a quite different situation presented itself to me in the role of escort when I had to accompany German military personnel in their own staff car away from the shelter of Tac, through mile after mile of the outside world, in which there were many hostile British and American troops, not only disinclined but forbidden to fraternise with the erstwhile enemy, and people of former occupied territory whose sufferings were reawakened by the sight of Nazi uniforms.

There were many moments of embarrassment for the occupants of the car when passers-by gave vent to their anti-Nazi feelings. As the Mercedes nosed its way cautiously over one Bailey bridge a grimy, red-faced sapper poked his chin over the door of the car and said through clenched teeth:

'Come on yer German bastards!'

Prolonged agony was endured when we had to follow the tail of an American truck crammed full of high-spirited GIs:

'Say Sarge, why don't you shoot that sonofabitch?'

This was just one of many uninhibited remarks flung at me. Some more soldiers along the road were heard to comment:

'That sergeant's asking for trouble.'

At the Dutch frontier the sentry could not read the English on the permit, and escorted us to the nearest CMP post. Dutch civilian policemen, reverting to their old underground tactics, directed the car along the wrong roads, until they saw the British uniform in the back and all too obviously changed their minds. Little Dutch boys shook their fists and shouted, 'Moffe, Moffe!' Other children waved from sheer force of habit.

It was good to see Holland again, decked out in celebration of victory. Orange streamers and red, white and blue flags fluttered from every building. In Deventer, Apeldoorn and Amersfoort the orange bunting stretched right across the road and made wheel-shaped designs across the public squares and market places. Banners bearing such inscriptions as:

WELCOME TO OUR LIBERATORS
THANK YOU ALLIES

made my German charges look thoughtful.

In Hilversum where German troops had resisted for two days after the surrender to Field Marshal Montgomery, the people were celebrating both their liberation and the victory in Europe. They seemed crazy with excitement, and reminded me of my first days in Brussels. While I was out walking in the evening through the streets of that beautiful modern town where I was struck by the elegance of the town hall and the radio station, people nodded and smiled at me from all sides, and a woman with a little boy stopped me. The small boy, at a given signal from his mother, read a long letter of appreciation and gratitude to the British troops for leaving their homes across the sea to come to liberate Holland. The Dutch would never forget that, the letter went on, and the British soldiers must know that they would always find a place in the grateful hearts of the Dutch people. It was a long, touching letter, full of expressions of gratitude and affection, and after reading it the boy put his hand in his mother's basket and drew from it a gaily painted red, white and blue box which he presented to me. The gift, a carved silver paper-knife, had been made by the boy's father in a factory where he was supposed to work for the Germans. Instead of concentrating on German weapons of war he had spent most of his time manufacturing souvenirs and trinkets for the long-awaited liberators. As we stood together talking, another small boy cycled past singing 'Tipperary' very self-consciously. Further down the street a respectably dressed old lady asked me for some food. A well-to-do Dutchman I met later explained to me that the only people in Hilversum with sufficient strength left to walk about were the rich who were able to patronise the Black Market:

'The poor are either dead or dying,' he added.

This Dutchman's wife had died two months earlier in a concentration camp; her only crime was to have a Jewish lodger. Towards the end of the war the Allies had pushed on to Berlin and by-passed north Holland, so that Hilversum was left as a pocket of German resistance. The Dutchman described these last few days as a Nazi reign of terror: people were deprived of the basic necessities of life and were constantly foraging for food; children did not go to school but went into the forest hoping to find something to eat; there was no coal, gas or electricity; wheat was ground in a coffee mill to make ersatz coffee; sugar beet was made into a pulp and, though horrible to eat, it constituted a main meal; others made themselves ill by eating tulip bulbs, and domestic pets disappeared in mysterious circumstances. Eighteen thousand people died of starvation. 'Not a scrap of food was left on 5 May when we were liberated.'

The German Headquarters consisted of a smart housing estate in the middle of a park-like district dotted with trees and shrubs. Leaving my German travelling companions in the care of General Blaskowitz, I spent a very comfortable night in the opulent billet of Number One Control Section. The car was to pick me up again at 4.30 a.m. Setting the alarm clock once more for 4 a.m., I curled myself up in the borrowed blankets and went to sleep. At 4 a.m. I was jerked out of my lethargy and switching off the alarm decided to luxuriate for five more minutes. When I opened my eyes again the time was 5.20 a.m.: panic ensued. Jumping from my bed straight into my clothes, I picked up my haversack and, minus wash and breakfast, dashed out into the street. As I was adjusting my gaiters by the kerbside the Mercedes hove in sight.

'Have you been here before?' I asked.

'No,' was the reply. 'So sorry if you were kept waiting.'

On the return journey the sun shone so brilliantly that it was decided to fold the hood back. Captain Tinius, either under the influence of the May sunshine or in a well-timed attempt to abolish non-fraternisation once and for all, started to become demonstrably friendly. He showed me photographs of his wife and baby, said that the English and

Germans were never meant to be enemies, that it was against his heart, putting his hand over his Iron Cross, to fight against people like me, and concluded by offering me a drink of milk.

The hostility which we had encountered on the outward journey had been so alarming that my German fellow travellers sought every route possible to avoid centres of population. We therefore made extensive detours through uninhabited stretches of country, isolated woods and by-ways, following tortuous country lanes to steer clear of the traffic and the insults on the main roads. Our evasive action was such that the route took us in a zig-zag pattern round the craters in a bombed airfield. When the car reached a delightful village by the name of Essen we decided, appropriately enough, that it was time to eat. Lieutenant-Colonel Friedel wandered away to a farmhouse to wash, while the rest of us munched our various sandwiches. Passing lorry-drivers gazed in bewilderment at the sight of a British sergeant eating sandwiches by the side of the road with German officers. It must have looked a strangely assorted party. When our hunger had been appeased we climbed into the car again and rolled on through village after village along empty roads. Captain Tinius, still in a confiding mood, begged to be allowed to see his wife and baby who had been evacuated to a small hotel in a village through which we must pass. When we reached the village it was obvious that the British army had taken over the hotel. I enquired of the whereabouts of the former occupants of the hotel and was told that they were all living in a house across the courtyard. Leaving Captain Tinius to see his family I made the interesting discovery that the sappers with whom I had joined up in 1940 and lived for two years were billeted in the hotel. We exchanged memories and they gave me an excellent tea.

Captain Tinius was in high spirits for the rest of the way back. After leaving this village of Bispingen near Soltau we soon left the by-ways and lonely hamlets and rejoined the main stream of traffic on the Lüneburg road. Here in the heat and the dust I dozed off, only to be awakened by the bumps over the Heath. Since yesterday we had travelled over nine hundred kilometres, nearly six hundred miles. I had felt, for a brief interval, what it was like to be a liberator again.

One extraordinary occurrence on this journey gave me the briefest of insights into the experience of being a German confronted by the hostility of the British, then being instantaneously greeted as a friend and ally (recalling memories of a Dundee power station and a similar reception by the Scots). This happened when a determined infantryman armed with a Sten gun jumped with legs astride in front of the car, the gun pointed threateningly at us. While we were thus held at gunpoint a British sergeant appeared. I showed him my pass.

'You have to thank your lucky stars your name is Sergeant Kirby,' he said.

'Why?' I asked.

'Because I am Sergeant Kirby too. No German spy would have cooked that up.'

On 18 May I was one of a fortunate group of men given a forty-eight-hour leave at the newly established Rest Camp at Lübeck. On our journey northwards we passed column after column of German prisoners on the road: some walking, some in lorries, others in horse-drawn vehicles. In these convoys there were many strange kinds of transport, including mobile kitchens with chimneys smoking and gas-driven trucks with their fuel on trailers. But it must be said that for eccentricity not even these conveyances rivalled the Tac HQ procession with its mobile church, the idiosyncratic black Daimler with the inward-sloping windscreen, and the despised 'iron lung'.

The weekend in Lübeck was a time of restful calm and relaxation in the midst of our tormented existence, with only the occasional reminder of recent horrors. The building in which we were billeted had been either a luxury hotel or the home of some wealthy industrialist. So great was my feeling of release from the pressures and uncertainties of war that on arriving in this elegant environment I went round switching all the lights on. There was an extensive flower garden with a smooth well-kept lawn running down to a lake. I enjoyed the hours spent on the landing-stage at the bottom of the garden, reading and gazing at the sparkling water, then canoeing and exploring the backwaters between the smart houses with their neat gardens. On the surface Lübeck appeared to have emerged unscathed from the war, but the scars were there. Most of the people wore wooden expressions, yet there were efforts, especially amongst German girls, to break through the restricting non-fraternisation barrier. Everywhere there were groups of British soldiers chatting, laughing and flirting with young German women. Talk among the troops on leave was dominated by the topic of non-fraternisation and its possible early collapse as a result of almost universal infringement. Children were the first to storm this barricade. On Whit Monday, a day of glorious sunshine with fresh summer breezes, we were tempted to take a boat out again. We ventured into some of the less frequented channels where willow trees trailed their branches in the water and fish were clearly visible in the depths. When we were walking in the town many of the girls tried to evade our looks, but here on the water, passing us in their canoes, girls smiled at us and some offered us sweets. Two little German boys (Wolfgang and Hermann) tacked on behind us in their rubber dinghy, spending most of the afternoon in tow, thus making nonsense of the war so recently ended and of the official frigidity with which we were commanded to treat the enemy.

There was, however, no complete escape from the war and its miseries even in beautiful, peaceful Lübeck. In the town, notices posted outside newspaper offices asked for news of lost relatives, and in shop windows photographs of the concentration camps and other Nazi atrocities were displayed with the object of arousing feelings of revulsion and guilt in the local population. Similar reminders of wartime affliction were noticeable on our journey by Troop Carrying Vehicle (TCV) into Travemünde, where we had a quick dip in the icy waters of the Baltic.

Back in Lübeck the sound of the cuckoo punctuated the quiet of the evening, but this restful mood was disturbed by the thought that we had to pack our kit and board the transport for our return to camp at Lüneburg.

And so my return to Tac in this newly-fledged, unaccustomed peace involved another series of escort duties, mostly in the company of Captain Tinius, sometimes with General Gareis, with the object of bringing yet more German staff into the employment of our recently established German camp. I therefore became officially permitted and even obliged to fraternise. Some men may have been able to carry out these duties and, at the same time, convey an attitude of continuing hostility or at least of disapproval. I have never been very good at these stern postures, even as a teacher, and though not going as far as cultivating the friendship of Captain Tinius, I never ceased to feel sorry for him as another suffering, fallible human being, with his long exile from his family, his uprooted wife and little girl, and his homelessness. At least we remained companionable to each other, forced as we were to share for hours the restricted space of a car and picnics by the roadside. He could possibly have seen that I also suffered with him the insults and humiliations of those journeys, until of course it was realised by some of the bystanders that I was an escort and not an erstwhile enemy. These experiences were a sore trial for him, but they were not very enjoyable for me either. His sensitivity to the local hatred was no less remarkable than his seeming ignorance of the reasons for it, so efficiently had Dr Goebbels done his propaganda work. Distasteful though it was to drive through angry crowds of shouting, cursing, spitting, fist-shaking people, I did of course have the moral support and tangible back-up of the official permit bearing the necessary face-saving words.

The resumption of duties at Tac HQ involved the usual disregard for what would now be considered normal or 'social' hours of work or, expressed negatively, unsocial hours were the norm. A telephone message at 2.30 a.m. informed me of the arrival of another German officer and driver for whom sleeping accommodation had to be found. In pouring rain two tents were put up and an untimely nocturnal visit to the disgruntled but philosophical quartermaster furnished them with beds and bedding. I had to be up again at 6.45 a.m. as escort for Captain Tinius.

On the 23 May came the news of Mr Churchill's resignation and the approaching end of the Coalition Government. A caretaker government was to take over until the General Election. Field Marshal Montgomery was nominated Commander-in-Chief of the British Occupying Forces in Germany.

Escort duties continued as did journeys connected with the delivery of German documents. Among these were pamphlets from Field Marshal Busch's Headquarters: 19,500 addressed to German civilians and 2,000 to soldiers, giving the latest information and instructions from Field Marshal Montgomery. Remnants of the German army were to be withdrawn into the northern peninsulas.

16

LIFE IN POST-WAR GERMANY

SCHLOSS OSTENWALDE

On 28 May 1945 Tac HQ moved into its permanent peace-time home, the idyllic rural backwater of Ostenwalde. An inspection of the Schloss and farmhouses showed that the furniture had been left intact and all the rooms scrupulously cleaned and tidied ready for occupation. Soon after this move my remaining companions in the Counter-Intelligence Detachment received postings to other units: Butch and Tony to Main HQ for liaison duties and Bob to HQ 43 Division as Sergeant Instructor in the Army Education Corps; Captain Thornton had already left and Dodger applied for a commission and was successful.

These departures left me alone again at Tac in charge of security, to which was added a multitude of official and unofficial chores. Excerpts from two of my letters home convey some idea of the harassing life which being a linguist with HM Forces in peace-time Germany involved:

2 June 1945
. . . Since last I wrote I have been so feverishly busy that correspondence of any kind has been out of the question for me. Scarcely have I finished breakfast than my name starts being shouted, and I am on the go all day. It is good to sit down in the evenings when that is possible. I was even dragged out of bed at 2.30 this morning to go to a farm where a party of Russians had shot two German farmers. In addition to my normal duties I am acting as the camp interpreter at present. I have to organise German labour at the château, give orders to gardeners,

carpenters, plumbers, blacksmiths, foresters, electricians, cleaners and the local baron. I must be in constant contact with the bürgermeister and the Military Government. I have to negotiate to provide billets for the troops, and it is my business to procure such things as water pipes, boilers, safety valves, thermometers, stopcocks, timber, nails, paint, brushes, furniture of all descriptions, curtains, carpets, and foodstuffs such as eggs, butter and milk. I must arrange for grass to be cut, roads to be swept and farm buildings to be tidied. I must keep an eye on civilian traffic on the road to prevent strangers from trespassing and issue passes to the chosen few who are allowed to work here.

In addition I have been called upon, together with Bob Forrest, to organise an Education Scheme for Tac. I am also a settler of local disputes between Nazis and anti-Nazis, and between Russians and Poles on the one hand, and Germans on the other. In other words I can manage to pass the time nicely without getting bored . . .

I have just received a letter from my Dutch friends – the 'Royal Needlewoman' and her husband – and they too want to visit us in England. Aren't we popular! Their whole family were so good to me during my stay in Eindhoven, and treated me so much as a son that I should like to repay their hospitality. The sister is getting married to a trooper from Hertfordshire, and the brother-in-law is married to a girl from Tavistock, so they intend to call on me on their way to see their relatives. . . .

Another letter dated 17 June 1945 gives a similar impression of a busy life:

. . . I am so busy now that I have very little time to myself. I have had to hide myself in Bob's billet for this afternoon in order to write you this letter. I am longing for leave and I hope my lucky day will come soon.

This work has been excellent for my German. In

addition to the more ordinary kinds of conversation I have had to make myself acquainted with all sorts of technical terms. For example I have to accompany the RE officer whenever he wants to requisition stores. In order to interpret for him I have to know the German words for such things as hasps, staples, rim-locks, shelf-brackets, iron and lead piping, S-bends, T-joints, lavatory cisterns, tongued and grooved timber, safety valves, stop cocks and other similar gadgets. Farmers talk in agricultural terms and I have to be *au fait* with root crops, cereals, fodder for the cattle, farm implements and all the usual farm activities of sowing, reaping, threshing and so on. Plumbers ask for conical screw joints, painters for cellulose paint or matt distemper, gardeners for antirrhinums, chrysanthemums, cucumbers and leeks, so my German is put to a severe test. The other day I had to act as interpreter at a summary of evidence in which one of the witnesses was a German woman. . . .

One of our private soldiers at Tac HQ had shot her friend and fellow-worker in the Schloss kitchen. This could have been disastrous for our reputation in the village had it not transpired that, in a playful mood the soldier had been teasing the woman by pointing the revolver at her and it had accidentally gone off. Her husband was in the German army and it would not be long before his demobilisation and return home. The local population were filled with apprehension about the effect of his reaction to the death of his wife at the hands of a British soldier. Needless to say the man responsible was sent away on detention.

COPING WITH DEFEAT

The immediate post-war period in Germany brought to light the mental and moral confusion of the people. The legacy of the Nazis was evident in the compulsiveness with which so many Germans denounced each other to us, the present power in the land. Expressions of hatred for the Nazis coupled with ingratiating flattery of the British way of life went along with sullen resentment and injured national pride. Some women openly expressed their wish to marry an Englishman but beneath these outbursts could be discerned that more urgent craving for a settled way of life which England seemed to promise.

Hunger and hardship drove many Germans to barter precious family heirlooms for cigarettes, a now dominant form of currency. Hungry children lined the railway banks where military leave trains were known to pass, in the hope that homegoing soldiers would part with their army rations and lunch packets. They did not wait in vain, as the troops could not resist the pathetic appeals of those thin faces and outstretched hands: chocolate, sandwiches, apples and biscuits were thrown in careless generosity from carriage windows. Cigarette ends were also scrambled for and collected.

In a country where obedience and allegiance to authority had been ingrained and automatic, there was now a degree of moral disintegration which suggested not only the disappearance of the external authority but also the atrophy, through disuse, of individual inner resources. Some young Germans confessed to attending a rally of Hitler youth in the afternoon and listening secretly to BBC radio in the evening, as if they thought that in confessing only lukewarm adherence to the Nazi cause and expressing an interest in the democratic one they might find favour with the reigning authority. Always this obsession with being approved of by those in power and never the individually-won engagement to a personal philosophy. But with minds conditioned from birth how could it be otherwise? Professions of support for the democratic way of life, and offers of friendship, though welcomed, were nevertheless marred by the shadows of the recent past. Equivocal too were the endless gifts for the Field Marshal – 'His Excellency' – handed in at the Schloss by petitioning Germans, some of whom had travelled long distances: bunches of flowers, fresh vegetables, eggs, a pot of home-made jam, a jar of honey, medicine for his sore throat. There was a steady stream of letters, all needing translation and all requiring the offices of a 'Good Samaritan', with whom 'His Excellency' as a man of God was equated: requests to provide employment, or living accommodation, or to intervene in family and neighbourhood quarrels. Field Marshal Montgomery's reputation as a practising Christian made him particularly vulnerable. There were repeated appeals to him from religious organisations to cleanse the country of the evils of nationalism, proclaim a nationwide return to God and re-establish a Christian Germany.

Some of the more straightforward requests I was able to deal with directly myself; in fact it was my function to do so: to grant or refuse the right of passage to farmers wishing to pass through our barriers to attend to work in the far corner of a field, to give or withhold permission to travel through the camp as a short cut to work, or to allow a doctor to visit a patient or a tailor to repair an officer's uniform.

On one memorable occasion I was ordered to fetch a tailor from a well-known firm of outfitters in Osnabrück to undertake alterations to the Chief's battledress. The large department store in Osnabrück was in ruins, but I found the tailor carrying on his business in a hotel outside the town. A summons to Ostenwalde, then established as a kind of substitute royal palace, could not be ignored so, asking if he could have time to change into his best suit, he disappeared for a quick transformation, climbed into the jeep and within the hour he and I were standing in Monty's bedroom where the Chief was already waiting, dressed in shirt and trousers. The interview was bright and crisp with no time-wasting preliminaries to put people at their ease. Monty, with his usual habit of saying things twice, sailed straight in:

'Sergeant Kirby, come here, come here. Does this fellow speak English?'

'No Sir.'

'Now listen to me. I'm going to have two more rows of medals, don't you know. Well there's no room for 'em. So this pocket will have to be dropped. Tell 'im. Can you cope?'

'Yessir.'

'Well cope.'

I then explained all this to the tailor, who was very quick to understand and respond. He replied that of course both pockets of the battledress blouse would have to be dropped.

Monty nodded: 'Quite so, quite so.'

The tailor then tentatively asked me, 'Can I make a suggestion to his Excellency?'

I approached the Chief with this request.

Monty agreed: 'Go ahead, go ahead.'

The tailor then made the following proposal: 'Your Excellency, the points of your collar are too long. They hide your medals. I make for you a neat, square collar and drop the pockets slightly. Then your medals will not be hidden.'

This was explained in English. Monty approved: 'Excellent, excellent.'

At this point an attendant officer, anxious to do his duty, intervened: 'Sergeant Kirby, don't you think you ought to be taking a few notes?' Monty swung round:

'Rubbish! The man knows his job.'

With that the business was agreed. We returned the next day with the finished battledress blouse beautifully pressed. Monty was delighted, and the same tailor received another order a month later to alter the Chief's trousers and give them a slimmer fit.

On another occasion I was asked to stand by to bring a German barber to cut the Chief's hair so I put on my best battledress and reported to the Schloss, but at the last moment it was decided to employ a British one. I suspected that the reason for this change of plan had more to do with the idea of a Prussian haircut than with security.

Amid the painful realities of defeat and destruction older Germans, with dogged determination, set about the almost superhuman task of rebuilding their country. For them it seemed as though sanity and salvation were to be found, not in philosophy or religion, but in WORK, sometimes hard, relentless, seemingly meaningless toil which demanded no critical thought but, with mind and hands fully occupied, provided escape and a kind of oblivion. In the towns we visited, groups of women carried baskets full of rubble from bombed buildings while others arranged piles of usable bricks in neat rows along the sides of the roads. I think of London, where ten years after the war acres of bombed sites were still being invaded by weeds and rosebay willowherb before being reclaimed by the builders. Even at Ostenwalde unpalatable work was done uncomplainingly by local villagers; their conscientiousness, it must be admitted, was easy to exploit in the new and uncomfortable relationship between victor and vanquished. Not many of the staff at Tac HQ took advantage of this situation and soon after the lifting of the ban on fraternisation we gained some measure of acceptance and trust in the village. In spite of the language barrier, the disreputable politics of Nazi Germany and the British tendency to feel superior and to hold themselves aloof, some positive relationships, if not friendships, did develop, and men found themselves invited into German homes, especially if there were common interests such as music, hobbies, professional or tradesmen's crafts, or a love of children or animals. It was hard, during this time of uncertainty in human encounters, to avoid the conviction that left to themselves ordinary human beings with no taste for power or domination, tend to move towards each other with some degree of sympathy or at least with curiosity, and that the movement towards hate is something that requires all the paraphernalia and technology of political propaganda to manufacture it. This may be naïve as it does not account for the misanthropy of some individuals, but this emotion is usually aroused by the spectacle of mankind in the mass and is usually a dislike of the anonymous crowd rather than of human beings as such. The war against Hitler and all the evils that he stood for was such a moral imperative that the slightest trace of friendliness towards Germans was felt to be a betrayal, and yet why the sense of relief when, after a few brief weeks, all barriers against fraternisation were lifted, if some deeper human essence were not involved?

Younger Germans – who are today's grandparents – seemed less addicted to the work ethic and less unthinkingly conscientious during the immediate aftermath of war. They were the casualties of the now defunct Nazi ideology and appeared completely disorientated, moving with mock humour from despair to flippancy. A young German woman, employed to work in our cookhouse, after complaining bitterly: 'Deutschland Kaput' said, 'But I like working for the English Army. We do a little bit of work, then we stop and have a cup of tea. Then we do a little more work and have another cup of tea. Then another little bit of work and another cup of tea. I like that. But when I worked for the German Army it was "Arbeit, Arbeit, immer Arbeit". I like the English way best.'

Confusion was most apparent in everyday morality where puritanism and permissiveness lived uneasily side by side. Priggish condemnation of American-style dancing, which prompted one German girl to say that if her father caught her jitterbugging he would shoot her, existed along with promiscuity and easy sex when the dancing was over.

It is not true that Germans have no sense of humour, or that they lack the ability to laugh at themselves, but like American humour it is different from ours. During the tenancy of the German High Command at Tac HQ on Lüneburg Heath after the surrender and my period of residence among them, I was often invited to their film shows, attended by the German officers and men on their staff. The films were mostly old German morale-boosting films, the nearest British equivalents being *The Dam Busters*, *The Way to the Stars*, or *Millions Like Us*, but more crudely and blatantly nationalistic. I was sitting in the tent surrounded on all sides by German soldiers enjoying their leisure, and whenever the Führer's name was mentioned in the film, or someone appeared on the screen giving a Nazi salute, the entire audience of German officers and men fell about and burst into shrieks of uncontrollable laughter. One of the films was called *Das Andere Ich*. It was about a factory girl who was so patriotic that she pretended to be her own twin in order to help Führer and Fatherland by working both a day and a night shift. This impossible enterprise proved to be so exhausting that she eventually collapsed on the factory floor, dying for her country in one final supreme sacrifice. Throughout this film the mirth of the audience knew no bounds and reached almost hysterical proportions. Officers and men were bent double in paroxysms of laughter. My own reaction was one of disbelief and embarrassment, but also of intense interest. As I came out of the tent on the Heath into the starry night my mind was full of questions. How single-minded had their allegiance been to the Hitler ideal? How threadbare was their belief in the Nazi cause? Was their disillusionment with Hitler a recent development, or was the dissatisfaction with their war effort – exemplified by the assassination plot of 20 July – a long-festering sore, finding an outlet now in a display of exaggerated hysteria? Did their love of Fatherland, true patriotism, remain intact in spite of defeat and betrayal? And was not this mockery rather than mirth, mockery not of their country but of the leaders who had failed them? Mockery too of the film itself with its transparent and unsubtle propaganda. How could a man laugh at his own country in its hour of suffering? It was obviously not laughter in which I, as an outsider, could join. A psychiatrist might have detected more than a hint of hysteria in all this seeming merriment, and I could not help feeling that tears could quite easily be an appropriate sequel to the laughter. I did not have long to wait, for soon after that film show not only did I have to listen to the outpourings of depressed individuals, but the news broke of the suicides, crashed cars and 'accidental' deaths of some of their military leaders, including all but one of the plenipotentiaries who had come to that historic tent on Lüneburg Heath to sign the surrender document.

Some Germans in Christian denominations had other feelings about Hitler's defeat but, having survived the war, had obviously not dared, during the Führer's lifetime, to express them openly. One Lutheran minister even went so far as to applaud the Allied victory and to say:

'If Germany had won, the world, including Germany, would have lost.'

Against this background of confusion and disorientation among civilians and military alike, life at Tac HQ continued in an atmosphere of rural and domestic calm. The menagerie was extended to include swans for the lake and peacocks for the lawn. Consignments of food had to be ordered for the various livestock both inside and outside the Schloss, and stabling had to be arranged for the horses. Sentries were posted on the road at the approach to the Schloss and sentry-boxes were required. I was sent on the inevitable errand to acquire them. In numerous journeys to former German army barracks only one sentry-box could be found. A second sentry-box would have to be made, so the village carpenter from Oldendorf was sent for. He was told to make an exact replica of the one already in position. When he had completed a magnificent wooden structure fit for Buckingham Palace I found him boring a hole in the side with bit and brace. I stopped him and asked him what he was doing. He replied:

'You said it was to be an exact reproduction of the other sentry-box.'

Sure enough there on the side of the original was a knot-hole of the exact dimensions of the hole being bored by our conscientious German carpenter. 'Obedience! Obedience!' had obviously been the watchword in German labour relations as in military discipline, but the love of work for its own sake was also a powerful driving force.

Among the many visitors to the Schloss with petitions of various kinds – and as the residence of Montgomery the administrator became more widely known they became a constant stream – there was one visitor who was more remarkable than the rest. This was Margarethe von Hase, widow of Lieutenant-General Paul von Hase, former Kommandant of the Berlin garrison and one of the conspirators in the plot of 20 July to kill Hitler. She had a gripping tale to tell. I invited her into the little gardener's lodge which, being by the entrance and the sentries, served me both as office and as billet.

When the assassination plot failed the Nazi government exacted a savage revenge. None of the conspirators or their families were to be spared. Thousands of German Liberals and Social Democrats were eliminated in the purge and there were wholesale arrests of innocent civilians whose only crime was to have been considered by the conspirators to be possible candidates for administrative office in the event of a successful coup. Most of these civilians knew nothing of the plot and were even unaware that their own names had appeared on a list of people chosen to work for the new administration. The exact numbers of those executed with or without trial will never be known.

Along with all the other relatives of the conspirators Margarethe von Hase was arrested, imprisoned and sentenced to death. She was miraculously released by the RAF, who bombed Berlin and destroyed the prison where she was held. She described how she escaped through the blazing inferno of the city, running down the centre of the road to dodge the scorching flames from burning buildings on each side of her. She made her way into the country to a farm where she had friends. They made a hiding place for her in the middle of a haystack, and there she remained, from autumn 1944 until May 1945 and the end of the war. Her two sons, one of nine and the other in his early teens, had also been arrested. The last she had heard of them was that they were in the hands of the Gestapo. Another escapee had told her that the older boy had been put into a concrete bunker and, with an electric light bulb between his eyes, had been given a third-degree interrogation. She was desperate to find her children and on 19 July, after many fruitless researches, had made the long journey to Ostenwalde to see Field Marshal Montgomery. At Ostenwalde he of course had no information concerning the whereabouts of what were then euphemistically called 'Displaced Persons', but his staff were able to put her in touch with the appropriate department at Main HQ. Her painful odyssey then took her to Bad Oeynhausen. As with so many of my stories, I never knew the outcome of this one. With some I was more fortunate and these will form the Epilogue to my narrative.

17

NON-FRATERNISATION

The Army scene within Tac HQ was less dramatic, still unpredictable, but on the whole more stable, with the usual church parades every Sunday, regular concerts and film shows in the barn newly converted into a comfortable cinema, and the setting up of the Study Centre where Army Education aimed to prepare men for their peace-time future. I was even called upon to give French, German and music lessons there. With the approach of colder weather, living accommodation for the men was provided by speedily erected wooden huts to replace the tents.

My powers as a linguist were also used and sometimes stretched to the utmost by a never-ending stream of letters addressed to the Chief. Many were from religious organisations and individuals in France, Belgium and Germany, urging Monty to restore universal love and brotherhood not only to the stricken Fatherland but to the whole planet. There were appeals from the people of Caen for permission to fête the Canadian army, and abundant correspondence from admirers, a passionate epistle from a Belgian countess, and a letter from two little Swiss boys, one an invalid. There was one appeal from a recently liberated victim from Buchenwald seeking employment, another from a Danish composer enclosing a march dedicated to Field Marshal Montgomery. I was required to play this to his staff on the elegant Schloss grand piano.

Most of the letters, like the majority of Germans we met, confessed ignorance of Nazi atrocities, and few indeed expressed any desire for the fulfilment of the Nazi ideal for which so many had fought. Some Germans wanted English to be recognised as a universal language, and in the vacuum left by the death of Hitler and the overthrow of his government some said they would welcome Montgomery as their new leader.

In addition to letters there were telephone calls. One, intended for the Chief, came through to me at the gardener's lodge by mistake. It was at 2 a.m. on 31 July and came in the form of a telegram. I wrote it down in the pitch dark with a blunt blue crayon on two plain postcards. The urgent voice said:

Pierre Laval left Barcelona in an aeroplane this morning with a German crew. It is quite possible he may try to land in British Zone. If so he and any other Frenchmen with him will be arrested and this HQ Inform immediately: 604 Military Government Detachment. The crew will be treated as POW. Inform aerodrome.

That was the end of the message and no more was said. I immediately rang Monty's staff in the Schloss, for whom the message was intended.

Never before or since that year in Ostenwalde has life provided me with opportunities to become acquainted with such a variety of people in so small a community, our village of Oldendorf and the nearby country town of Melle. It was like being minister of a parish in which every face was familiar, except that my role was not that of a pastor with his flock, but unpredictable. Most of the time I was a go-between in what was an occupied country, sometimes an amateur major-domo, a constrained master of ceremonies or an unobtrusive butler, a servant constantly on call, another Figaro. At other times I was invested with authority to summon people to the Schloss, for pleasant work or unpleasant labour, for consultation or for reprimand. The most rewarding errands were those concerned with the discovery and use of local skills for the benefit of the whole community, both military and civilian. This involved building some kind of working relationship with the bürgermeister, the village policeman, the pastor, the schoolmaster and the various artisans required for the work of settling in the new inhabitants of the Schloss, who happened to be the new administrative power in the land. One of our more colourful employees was the jocular chimney sweep in his traditional top hat, and among our persistent callers, both in person and on the telephone, were the baron and his family. For all these people I was the link between the Schloss and the village and always referred to as *der Dolmetscher*. For the many purchases required to refurbish the Schloss for its new tenants I acted as intermediary for the appropriate officer in charge of the buying and this necessitated interesting visits to the iron foundry, the boiler factory, the furniture factory, the silk factory, the wallpaper factory, the mattress factory and the rubber factory. One of the most fascinating visits was with a group of men from our Study Centre in the name of Army Education. This was to a match factory on the edge of a pine forest, where we actually watched the progress of huge pine trees to their final destination as boxes of matches.

Though so much of my time was taken up with interpreting and running errands I could not, for a moment, neglect my main function which was that of Counter-Intelligence Sergeant responsible for the security of Tac HQ and its Chief. This is where I came in, alone at the beginning and alone at the end. Security was an ever-present preoccupation even in this small, rural community, seemingly desirous of living on peaceable terms with the occupiers, because there were incidents. As time went on friendly gatherings and parties with Germans became more frequent and widespread, among the men first, then the officers, but here and there a few warning signals alerted us to be on our guard. In spite of the 'Frat Dances', the invitations for Christmas and birthday parties, the gifts of fruit, eggs and cake, the drinks of schnapps and home-made wine, the musical at-homes with accordion and flute solos and dancing, the spirit of rebellion was something to be reckoned with from time to time. For example on 22 August when Monty's aeroplane crashed, water was discovered in the petrol and with it a suggestion of sabotage. After this incident, in addition to tighter security, the airfield was floodlit. Then there was the swastika painted on the road, the inscription on the tower in the forest behind the Schloss:

'Unter mit den Allierten. Es lebe Deutschland'
Down with the Allies. Long live Germany

There were isolated attacks on our troops at night: a brick thrown at one of our jeep drivers, and one of our men shot in the neck at point-blank range at a 'Frat Dance'; he was rushed to hospital and survived. These incidents were few and far between, and on our side we received unsolicited denunciations and reports from self-appointed informers. There were the familiar tales of flashing lights, all of which had to be investigated, usually in the small hours. There was Fritz Grabsch who came to me in great secrecy to warn the Field Marshal of the formation of the 'Werewolves' from the ranks of the SS and the RAD. He had been moved to come by his hatred of the Nazis and his anxiety over the threat to the life of Field Marshal Montgomery. He went on to speak slightingly of different village personalities including the bürgermeister and the baron's family, of whom I should beware. He had heard of a plot by the baron's daughters to cut off the hair of German girls who gave information to the Military Government. During the interview he was extremely fidgety, kept looking over his shoulder, was worried by the open window and said '*das Fenster stört mich*' ('The window disturbs me'). Three weeks later he disappeared as mysteriously as he had come.

I must admit that I was often as worried by the open friendliness as by the surreptitious resistance. Yet we had Monty's approval for fraternisation, once it was realised that the alternative was impossible to implement. It had been

Monty's custom throughout his campaign to trust the British soldier, for whom he expressed a high regard, to take him into his confidence, to help him follow the progress of the current campaign and to explain the further steps to be taken for winning the war. These talks were given to us regularly both by the Chief himself and by his staff, with the aid of maps pinned up on the side of a truck. I remember with a tremor of excitement the talk given to our tiny, hushed HQ on the eve of 'Overlord' and our never-to-be-forgotten departure for Normandy. Now that peace had arrived Monty tried the same tactic with the defeated Germans, giving them a message in simple, straightforward language, explaining why the normally friendly British soldier was not smiling at them. This was the first part of non-fraternisation. The total ban on friendly association with our former enemy was gradually relaxed in stages, starting with the children. From 12 June we were officially permitted to do what we had already been doing: to talk to and play with the children. There was a further loosening of the regulations when from July the troops were allowed to talk to Germans in public places, but not to go into their homes. Another stage was reached when in September Monty successfully raised the issue in the Control Council and the ban on fraternisation was lifted. Billeting of the armed forces with Germans and marriage with them were, however, forbidden. In my diary I noted:

Saturday 14 July: The ban of fraternisation is lifted.
Sunday 15 July: Fraternisation is now in full swing. I saw soldiers talking gaily to groups of civilians who were airing themselves in the cool of the evening at their front doors.

In my work as interpreter for the Schloss I was, of course, obliged to enter German homes, months before the ban was lifted. It seems to be in the nature of restrictions that, as soon as the restraints are off, human nature goes to the opposite extreme. From September onwards parties, dances and musical evenings became a regular feature of life in Oldendorf, in nearby Melle and in Osnabrück. On 8 September the dance hall in Osnabrück was crowded with British soldiers and their German partners while barefooted children thronged the window-sills.

Some of our men, however, could not go along with the current mood of togetherness and forgetfulness. With or without resentment of the Germans there was for them an unseemliness, a loss of dignity in this all-too-hasty transition from foe to friend. We had so recently seen the victims of the Nazi holocaust and had forged deep and lasting relationships with those who had suffered and fought against tyranny. What would they think of us? Yet this was 'peace'.

I continued to be haunted by memories of Inge, of Maria and of the brave and noble Nandy Gennotte – I still am.

18

TAC HQ IN PEACETIME

It is possible that Monty's concern over the unnaturalness of prolonged non-communication (*le silence de la mer*) with those among whom the troops were living, whether former enemies or not, may have been intensified by some visible signs of strain affecting individuals at his own Tac HQ. The almost monastic isolation imposed upon men with no vocation for it, worries about wife and family after months without leave, and unresolved feelings about our German neighbours were beginning to take their toll in different ways according to differing temperaments, from open grumbling on the one hand to mute depression on the other. At 6 a.m. one chilly autumn morning the camp was startled by rifle fire from the direction of the newly erected ablutions. The bullet holes in the woodwork of the hut and the blood splashed on the ceiling and the lamp were not the work of a hostile intruder but of one of our own comrades: 'Jock' had shot himself.

Apart from the brief experience of Brussels – even there we were stationed on the rural outskirts – our camp had always been in lonely places. Some could be described as desolate, some were buried in deep forest-gloom, some were idyllic. In such a quiet, secluded corner of Westphalia as Ostenwalde, ideal for monks and hermits and those of us who enjoyed communing with nature, it soon became clear that it was important for the majority of members of HM Forces to have access to facilities for recreation and diversion after the daily routine of army duties. These were not necessarily made available by the freedom to fraternise, so efforts were made to supply these amenities within the camp area itself. We had our football field and swimming pool, hunts were arranged for the officers after negotiation with Herr Heuer, the forester, and Monty himself was sometimes seen playing tennis in the summer and skating on the lake in the winter. There were regular concerts of classical music provided by German instrumentalists and singers, and popular entertainments by other performers, including a group who called themselves 'The Swallows'. It was strange and somehow uncomfortable to listen to German artists singing the current popular songs of the Allies: 'Beautiful Dreamer', 'Goodnight Sweetheart', 'J'attendrai', and doing 'The Lambeth Walk'. There were also visits from ENSA, among whom Geraldo and his Band were the most warmly received, and regular showings of some of the most recent films, including *Henry V* and *The Way to the Stars*. The Study Centre catered for our intellectual and educational needs, as well as paving the way for demob.

In addition to these domestic arrangements there were short leaves to the Rest Centres at Lübeck, the Harz mountains where we went ski-ing and tobogganing, and the Dummersee. There were excursions to Brussels and Paris, and conferences at 30 Corps Church House in Einbeck with trips to Göttingen and other places of interest.

Life was therefore not dull, but it was life in limbo, life in a waiting-room, in suspense until real life began again with the great day of demobilisation. For many it was with mixed feelings that this long-awaited day dawned, at different times for different men, and I felt a great sadness, in spite of the jolly farewell parties, as one after the other my comrades left, most of whom I would never see again.

My own date for demob was 19 February, so I would spend another Christmas at Tac, my sixth in the army, but events were to take a sombre turn before that. At 9.30 a.m. on 21 November Driver Menzies, our new young jeep driver, picked up my mate Ted Allen and me at the office to collect a new CI 15 cwt truck from I. Corps Field at Bad Salzuflen. It was a misty morning, bleak and raw. As the back seat of the jeep was going to be piercingly draughty we decided to put a wooden plank across the two front seats, so that we could all three sit together for warmth, shielded by the windscreen. But whoever sat in the middle was going to have a very uncomfortable journey with no back support, so we tossed up and I lost. Ted had the passenger's seat and our driver, of course, was in the other firm seat. I did as best I could in a crouching posture, sandwiched between the other two men trying, at the same time, to avoid becoming entangled with the gear lever and being jerked backwards into the space between the seats. At the time, I never realised how fateful for all of us those seating arrangements were.

We had been travelling for about an hour and at a cross-roads in Eilzhausen came to a stop at the traffic lights. A convoy of Belgian Army lorries crossed from left to right in front of us. I remember counting eight lorries. Then the lights changed; we started forward and were nearly in the centre of the crossing when the driver of the ninth and last Belgian lorry, possibly anxious not to be left behind at the lights, put his foot on the accelerator and sliced through us at speed. The next thing I remember is lying in the road with an acute pain in my left side and having great difficulty in breathing. I recall being carried gently by a group of Germans into a nearby house and coming to rest on a sofa. I never lost consciousness. In the ambulance that took us to the 23rd Scottish General Hospital at Wittekindshof near the village of Volmerdingsen, I was on the lowest stretcher and Ted on the one above me. The blood from his fractured skull spurted over me until it covered my face. By the time we reached the hospital I was so saturated in Ted's blood that, as I was told later by the nurses, they thought I was the worst casualty; but it was Ted who died.

As the jeep somersaulted with the full force of the impact on the passenger's side, Ted's skull was the first part of him to hit the ground. Driver Menzies broke all his limbs and was badly burned. I was saved by my uncomfortable travelling position, cushioned as I was between the bodies of my two companions, and escaped with six broken ribs and a broken wrist. I subsequently heard from our breakdown gang that our jeep had caught fire, having been cut in half and was picked up in two completely separate pieces scattered several yards apart. I never knew what happened to the Belgian driver. Soon after the accident there was one day when I had more than the usual number of visitors from Tac. They had come for Ted's funeral, but I had not been told that he had died.

Life in hospital followed a strict routine not unlike the rituals of a peace-time army, with daily inspections and standing to attention while the colonel, followed by his retinue in descending order of rank, went on a tour of the wards. I did my best, propped up by six pillows, to sit to attention. Those patients with no limbs to stand on could only tense their facial muscles while being inspected. After one of these inspections matron came storming back to my bed:

'Sergeant Kirby, the colonel could not help remarking that the tapes of your pillow-cases were visible. He wasn't very pleased.'

With my six pillows that meant a lot of tapes.

'My heart bleeds for him,' I replied.

'Don't be impertinent,' said matron, 'and next time see to it that your tapes are towards the window and well tucked in.'

Reveille was at 5 a.m. when those of us unable to get out of bed were washed by a male nurse. This drill was followed by breakfast, after which matron and sister came round the wards to make sure that all was ship-shape before the doctor did his rounds. There was another three-minute warning before the colonel's inspection, to give us time to remove any objects which might give offence.

Apart from these minor irritations there was a tranquillity about this ordered life which was a relief from the unpredictable scramble and ferment of much of my work at Tac. Within the well-regulated timetable of every day there was enough leisure to think, to read, to draw, to talk to fellow-patients and get to know them. There was time also to notice the changing colours of the sky through the hospital windows. One morning in early December the sun was a blaze of copper. On another morning we woke up to look out upon a world covered with snow. It had arrived so silently during the night and it sparkled from every field and fence and rooftop in the early sunlight. Illness and disablement, however temporary, gives the patient an opportunity to discover who his friends are. There were many visitors from Tac who travelled the long distance with presents of fruit, biscuits, ham rolls, chocolate, cigarettes, bottles of lemonade, books, magazines, writing paper, records and such imaginative gifts as drawing materials, my own diary which I had left behind in the camp, and a cake made by Monty's chef. Among the German villagers Herr Meyer, the farmer, sent apples and eggs, the bürgermeister's wife, Frau Moseler baked me a cake, Herr Horst sent a box of apples, biscuits and a chicken, and from the Brandhorst family came a Christmas tree.

I shall always remember with gratitude Lance-Corporal Dicky More who hitch-hiked all the way from Tac many times, kept me generously supplied with fruit, books, records and messages from the village, stayed with me and took the doubtful chance of finding transport on the road to give him a lift back, sometimes in the dark. One day when I was up and able to walk about he took me to see Ted's grave and the graves of four other colleagues from Tac, including that of Jock who had shocked us all by committing suicide. Driver Menzies was not told about Ted's death until it was felt he was strong enough to receive the news.

The main occupations of convalescent patients were reading, playing draughts and cards, doing jigsaw puzzles, listening to records in the Recreation Room and waiting on other patients. One day a nineteen-year-old sapper was brought into a private ward suffering from severe injuries as a result of being thrown off his motor cycle by a wire stretched across the road. It was a miracle that he was not decapitated by this deliberate act of 'peace-time' sabotage, but he had to have one leg amputated below the knee. The after-effects of this operation and his solitary confinement in a private ward made him so depressed that sister suggested my bed be moved into his room. I was sorry at first to miss the company and liveliness of the general ward, but Sapper Jones and I soon became friends. He gradually cheered up and with the approach of Christmas we busied ourselves making our own Christmas cards and decorations, silver stars cut out of sheets of tin and coloured balls of cotton wool. Every night we wrote 'poems' to the nurses.

Life was pleasant. Nurses came round with sprigs of mistletoe to hang over our beds. The German girls sang carols, including *'Heilige Nacht'*, as they worked and sometimes the RAMC band gave a concert in the afternoon with a mixed repertoire of Mozart, Schubert, Dvořák and Liszt, followed by ten minutes of 'Swing'. There were also film shows and it was in hospital that I saw John Mills, Michael Redgrave and Rosamund John in *The Way to the Stars*.

My friends were more than generous in their gifts and their visits to the hospital and I was moved by their kindness and by the sympathy of the people of Oldendorf. This gave me more food for thought about the war, about the savage necessity to win it while it lasted, the ease with which people seemed to forget it once it was over, and the abrupt transition from the tragic to the commonplace which characterised the experiences of those days.

Christmas came and I was discharged from the hospital just in time to be cheered by the festivities of the Sergeants' Mess and indulged by the hospitality of a German family. The Schloss looked more peaceful than ever against its background of densely packed trees covered in hoarfrost. We had our church service and later that day a sprightly Field Marshal Montgomery gave us his seasonal message before the Christmas concert. The camp would soon learn that their Chief had been made a Viscount in the New Year's Honours List. For many of us life seemed more hopeful and the war a nightmare soon to be forgotten. For others it was different. On my last day in the hospital I said goodbye to Sapper Jones after cutting out a tin man and woman to hang next to the mistletoe over his bed when Driver Menzies was carried into the room. He was very weak and still asking after Ted Allen.

Though I had been told by Major Coverdale not to work, I was obliged to resume my duties on 27 December as the queue for workers' passes lengthened and there was nobody else to speak German and do the vetting. There were eighty-five passes to be issued and some of the Germans had to queue for two hours.

Life at Tac continued with these customary duties of checking visitors, issuing passes, playing the piano in church, investigating complaints by one German against another, and going out as interpreter on the usual excursions to workshops and factories to buy things for the Schloss and the camp. There were also my daily visits to the Medical Centre for physiotherapy and breathing exercises, but all these routines came to a full stop when security was threatened. There were occasional raids on suspected Nazi hide-outs, on families suspected of Black Market dealings with British or American troops, or on so-called 'houses of ill-repute'. Most of these raids were in places several miles away from Oldendorf, which was generally peaceful and law-abiding. I did, however, receive a report about a village 'terrorist' who later burst into tears under interrogation, and was required to question another, arrested by the village policeman, Herr Strobach, for saying, 'It's about time the Russians came here.' Another puzzling incident was the fire which broke out mysteriously in the Schloss greenhouse, burning all the Chief's plants.

Apart from these and other false alarms the domestic life of Tac HQ was smooth and uneventful. One happy event was the return to camp of Driver Menzies, who had managed to pull through and though walking with a stick, was on the road to recovery and a speedy release from the army.

In spite of our geographical seclusion Tac HQ as the

nerve centre of the war in Northern Europe was in permanent touch with world events. Other ranks regularly received army newsletters about international affairs, including happenings at home and our own General Election. Labour's victory was attributed by reporters to the Armed Forces' vote, and given the war-weariness of many men this was no doubt true. On 2 August we listened on the radio to the results of the Potsdam Conference on the post-war settlement of Europe, and on 7 August the entire camp was awestruck and obsessed by the news of the explosion of the first atomic bomb over Japan. Though there was obvious relief in the realisation that this would mean the end of the war in the Far East, our many lengthy discussions stressed the point that from now on the world was going to be a much more dangerous place. One sergeant remarked:

'How typical of human beings that the first thing scientists do with all their atomic research is to make a bloody bomb!'

On 8 August we heard that the Russians were declaring war on Japan, and at 2 p.m. on 10 August the news came through that Japan would surrender on condition that the Emperor remained Head of State. The news of Japan's surrender was announced at 1 a.m. on 15 August and VJ-Day was to be celebrated on this day and the day after. The Chief announced a holiday for Tac on 16 August. An illuminated V sign appeared on the top of the tower in the woods at Ostenwalde, and on Sunday 19 August Monty had a special church parade and a thanksgiving service for victory.

19

DEMOBILISATION

On Sunday 17 February 1946 I played the piano at our Tac Church service for the last time. In spite of my imminent demob there was no easing of the pressure of work, and on the 18th, the eve of my ultimate departure from Tac HQ and the army, I was vetting Germans who had applied for work on the B115 airstrip, issuing *Fragebogen*, and dashing off to Bad Oeynhausen, Bünde and Altenmelle to collect goods ordered for the camp. My last night was spent at Tac cinema watching a film called *29 Acacia Avenue*, starring Gordon Harker and Betty Balfour.

The next morning, 19 February, I began my round of farewells with the men's and sergeants' messes, then ended up at the Schloss saying goodbye to Major Coverdale, Major O'Brien and Captain Henderson, Monty's ADC. Kirby's last salute was a memorable and painful affair. Standing to attention in front of Major Coverdale in the elegant Mozartzimmer I made up my mind to give him the salute to end all salutes. As my arm flew up with strict military precision – the longest way up and the shortest way down – I felt a sharp pain across my knuckles as my hand made violent contact with the major's elegant standard lamp. Like a meteor this handsome piece of furniture described a graceful, luminous arc about two feet above my head and, still attached to its delicately carved wooden stand, crashed to a crumpled, shapeless heap on the floor. With burning cheeks and a muttered apology I did what I could to pick up the pieces, then beat a hasty, unmilitary retreat. For the whole of my journey homewards by truck to Bad Oeynhausen and to the station at Osnabrück I felt covered in confusion. The whole incident was reminiscent of the worst gaffes of Laurel and Hardy or Charlie Chaplin. Meeting one of my ex-army friends in London months later I told him of my embarrassment. He said that the episode had become one of Major Coverdale's favourite after-dinner stories and kept the officers' mess in fits of laughter for many days afterwards.

Getting demobbed was a lengthy business. The journey home was to take a whole week, from 19 to 26 February. As our train drew into Münster I gave my sandwiches to a hungry-looking German boy who devoured them then and there. We followed the familiar route through Wesel, Nijmegen with its bitter memories, Roosendaal, Brussels and Tournai. It began to snow and it was at Tournai that troops bound for demobilisation were eased by degrees out of their military chrysalis into a foretaste of forthcoming civilian attractions. There was the Arcon prefab exhibition house, one of the new 'homes for heroes', to which we were introduced by an ATS guide, the Bowler Hat Club decorated with murals depicting homeland scenes, cafés blaring out popular British and American dance music and shacks with notices advertising 'Egg and chips any time'. From Tournai we moved off at 5 a.m. to Calais Transit Camp then, after a calm crossing, to Folkstone and Shorncliffe Barracks. Here the great army striptease began in earnest. I was divested of my webbing, my gascape, blankets, mess tins and water bottle, my companions for six long years. The film showing that evening before our final release was, appropriately Noel Coward's *In Which We Serve*, but instead of going to see it I walked along the sea front from Shorncliffe to Folkestone past the brilliantly-lit Grand Hotel. I had supper in a small fish-and-chip shop in Sandgate then climbed back up the dark hill path to the barracks.

On my last day in the army I got up at 7 a.m. and had breakfast. It was snowing and raining hard as the lorries moved off to Shorncliffe station. On arrival at Victoria we were taken in loaded TCVs in pouring rain to Albany

Barracks, Regent's Park. I waited in a draughty MT Bay in a biting wind, listening for my Zone number. After handing in my baggage I had dinner in a long mess hall, then in the Arrival Rest Room waited for my number to be called. From there I was ordered to the Routine Section Waiting Room where we were told by a sergeant what to do in our first week of demob. Then we queued up upstairs to go past ten tables where we were issued with various documents, including Health and Ration Cards and our pay. Mine was £12 3s. I bought fifty-six days' worth of cigarette and sweet rations in the NAAFI, then waited for transport in the Departure Waiting Room where I whiled away the time at the piano. A lorry then took us to Olympia where we formed another queue, were measured, and helped ourselves to civilian suits, raincoats, shirts, ties, hats, shoes, socks and studs. It was snowing heavily as I came out. On the crowded lorry to Earls Court I realised I had left all my NAAFI rations behind. By the time I reached home about 6.30 in the evening the snow lay thick.

It was good to have supper at home, to talk, to unveil my treasures, to have a hot bath and go to bed in pyjamas. Going to London next day I retrieved my NAAFI rations which had been securely packed and locked up for me. Those last days, however tedious the waiting and queueing, showed me how efficient British Army organisation could be. In this respect comparisons could fairly be made between demob and D-Day.

20
EPILOGUE

After the first excitement of demobilization there were many adjustments to be made to the changes involved in living as a newborn civilian. It meant the end of a life within a community circumscribed by familiar rules and rituals, and the loss of the sense of comradeship built up between human beings who for years had shared the same living conditions, the same rough journeys to strange places, the same hardships and endured the same frustrations of army discipline relieved by the same grim and ribald humour. Six years of an established way of life – only the last two of which are recorded in this book – vanished overnight and the bewildered soldier found himself getting used to new freedoms and new responsibilities; surrounded by family and friends who had also experienced the war but in very different circumstances, and by others who had somehow escaped the worst discomforts and with whom there were few points of contact. With his softer clothes and lighter footwear he now joined these and others in the great anonymous mass of people who were determined to put the war behind them and give first priority to a life they could call their own.

I missed my comrades and for a few years after my release kept up a correspondence and a number of meetings and visits which, in the course of time, and as the result of diverging interests and associations, sadly died, as did some of these comrades themselves. Others I never saw or heard of again.

But I have seen again or been in touch with a number of the friends made during the campaign in Europe. I returned to teaching in 1946 and, after working in three different schools found myself in 1952 in the School of Education (then known as the Education Department) at Goldsmiths' College, training teachers. In our primary education department we had a course for overseas students, among whom were a number of Roman Catholic priests and nuns preparing themselves for teaching in the mission field. In one of my education groups, in addition to British students, I had five German nuns and seven priests: four Canadian, one Swiss, and two Dutch. The two Dutchmen were Father Elstgeest and Father Kuipers. One afternoon I was giving Father Kuipers a tutorial. I marked his essay, we discussed it, then settled down for a chat. Father Kuipers asked:

'Do you know my country, Mr Kirby?'

'Oh yes,' I replied with enthusiasm.

'When was that?'

'During the war. In fact the very first Dutch person I ever met was a child, a boy of nine.'

'Tell me about it.'

I then went on to describe the incident referred to earlier in this book about the small boy who introduced me to his father when I was investigating a camp site. I had got to the middle of my story when Father Kuipers, leaning forward, placed his hand on my arm and with great excitement burst out, 'And that is the moment when I got on your motor bike!'

He had never known the name of the soldier who gave him a ride, and it had never dawned on me that the young Catholic priest and the little Dutch boy could be one and the same person. In Holland the name Kuipers is as familiar as Cooper in England. His name was Paul, but at college he was always referred to as Father Kuipers never as Father Paul. I was completely taken aback by this coincidence.

In 1976, Vic Kelly, the Dean of the School of Education, invited me to meet the managing director of Harper and Row, his publishers. We arrived at their office in Covent Garden and there standing at the top of the stairs to greet us was the managing director himself, Paul Kuipers. I had not known of his movements since he left college to be a missionary in Africa, so after an impressive lunch I ventured to say to Mr Kuipers when we were alone:

'I should like to ask you a question.'

He laughed.

'I know what it is. Whatever happened to *Father* Kuipers?'

'Yes.'

'Well I blame Goldsmiths'. I fell in love with one of your students. While I was in Africa I found it difficult to concentrate on what I was supposed to be doing. The bishop became aware of it and I found I could no longer remain a priest, though I am still a Catholic. I came to England and married her. We have four children.'

'But how did you get into the publishing business?'

'Through a commercial traveller. He came to the school where I was teaching and when I complained to him how hard it was to keep a wife and four children on a teacher's pay he said, "Why not join us?" I did and here I am! Managing Director!'

He has since moved on to greater affluence in the world of publishing. This meeting had been arranged between Mr Kelly and Mr Kuipers who this time knew of my existence at Goldsmiths' College, but for me it was another remarkable coincidence.

Going back again to the years after demobilisation but before my meeting with Father Kuipers there were other echoes from the past. I went back to Holland as a civilian, staying with Inge and her younger brother Hilmar and they paid return visits to England. They had moved to Leiden then to Oestgeest after the starkest family tragedy made the memory of Eindhoven more than they could bear. Inge's father, a leader of the Dutch Resistance, survived many dangers to see the liberation of Eindhoven, but felt compelled to go on a hazardous mission back into occupied northern Holland. As an employee of Philips, Eindhoven, one of his covert activities was the despatch of illicit radio transmitters to the Resistance. They were hidden in a variety of ingenious ways, for example, secreted inside a lump of coal to be delivered in a marked sack among other sacks on a marked lorry. The Gestapo were waiting for him and he was executed. His son, Inge's elder brother, committed suicide and her mother became permanently insane. The reason for the suicide was not clear; whether through grief over his parents, or because the Gestapo were also after him, will never be known. The younger brother, Hilmar, took a positive direction and studied to become a psychiatrist, a profession which he now follows.

On Saturday 11 May 1946 I received a letter from Bernard Zweegers of Geldrop telling me of Maria's death in a road accident. Soon after our departure from Geldrop she had joined the Red Cross as a nurse. The driver of the ambulance in which she was travelling one night through bomb-shattered Germany could not see his way clearly and crashed over a bailey bridge into the valley below – Maria was killed. She had been the sweetest and most civilising influence on my restless army existence and we had made plans for coming together again after the war.

More remote from my own personal life was a news item which I read on 5 February 1948. It reported that Colonel-General Johannes Blaskowitz, one of the accused in the generals' war trial which began that day at Nürnberg, had committed suicide by leaping from the top floor of the court prison into the courtyard. The sixty-seven-year-old general broke away from a file of other prisoners on the third tier of the high catwalks surrounding the prison, clambered over a seven-foot protective wire, and hurled himself over it, landing on a tiled floor, thirty feet below – he died soon afterwards.

Blaskowitz commanded an army group which faced the British and Canadian armies in Western Europe. He was the officer who on 7 May 1945 escorted Major O'Brien, Chester Wilmot and myself to the Headquarters of the Wehrmacht at Flensburg on our journey to deliver the final terms of surrender to Field Marshal Keitel.

His suicide was the ninth by accused men in the

Nürnberg prison since the end of the war. It was to be followed by others. Field Marshal Keitel was hanged following his conviction as a war criminal at the trials.

In 1976 I received a picture postcard of a Dutch windmill with the strange message:

Before I die I should like to say good-bye to you, Elizabeth Schol (Van der Heijden) Royal Needlewoman to His Majesty King George VI of England [sic].

I pondered for a long while over these puzzling words. Was the postcard saying goodbye, or did she mean me to go and see her? I consulted a wise friend at college. He advised:

'She wants you to go. It's half term. What have you got to lose?'

The postcard had been clear and in faultless English, yet perhaps I should have guessed the awful truth that she was severely mentally ill.

At 7.30 p.m. on 28 May 1976, and following the advice of my wise, sensitive friend at Goldsmiths' College, I caught the Sealink train from Liverpool Street to Harwich. Though saddened by the circumstances and apprehensive about the nature of the unknown illness, I was spurred on by the thought that, after thirty-two years, I was going to see Elizabeth and Klaas again.

At 10 p.m. the *St George* left Harwich for the Hook of Holland, where I arrived at 5.30 a.m. There I boarded the 'Rhein Express' for Eindhoven, arriving shortly after 9 a.m. I had a cup of coffee in the station and at the office of VVV I booked a room, bed and breakfast with Mrs van den Heuvel at 137 Piuslaan, in order to be in the neighbourhood where Elizabeth lived. Mrs van den Heuvel had recently lost her husband and seemed pleased at the prospect of someone staying in the house. Her daughter called while I was there, no doubt with a view to inspecting her mother's new lodger, and kindly telephoned Elizabeth for me but without success. I therefore decided to make my own way to Elizabeth's flat at

Dr Poelspad 3, a few blocks away. She would not open the door. Her neighbour in No. 1, knowing that Elizabeth was at home, helped me by trying to telephone, but there was still no answer. I asked if I could contact Klaas, not knowing that he was living in another part of Eindhoven. We found his address in the telephone directory and fixed a meeting for me that evening. Coming out on to the landing I could tell that Elizabeth was in because I could see shadows moving on the ceiling through the glass of the door. I had no idea what kind of illness she was suffering from, but gradually the awful truth dawned as a small crowd of her neighbours began to collect outside her door.

Suddenly she opened the door wearing her dressing-gown, calle out:

'Norman!' and I walked into a flat littered with books, papers and unfinished meals, the remains of which were scattered on table, chairs and floor.

Elizabeth, eyes staring and hair dishevelled, had recognised me at once and was pleased to see me. She hugged and kissed me, saying she remembered me 'so well' and often spoke about me. Then in a whisper she confided that her flat was full of radioactivity. That was why her cheeks were red. It was in her hair and eyes and she could see it in mine too. She led me to the window and showed me where all this radioactivity was coming from – a bungalow over to the right where the owners received their orders from Sweden to afflict her in this way.

I tried to bring the conversation on to more solid ground and said I remembered her father and admired him for his courage as a leader of Christian resistance during the war. She then produced from her wardrobe shoe-boxes full of old photographs of her parents and family. I asked after her sister and she said she had nothing to do with her now as her sister was crazy. I thought of all those musical evenings with the family grouped round the piano, the accomplished flute and violin-playing.

The talk over photographs went on for a long time, then

she showed me other collections: stones, models of animals, scarves, a winter coat, several dresses and a Burberry raincoat 'from England'. I spent a long time with Elizabeth and wondered what possible good my visit had been to her – it had certainly depressed me. It was time to go: against her loud and pathetic protests I explained that I had a boat to catch, and when a rare interval occurred in her distracted outpourings I said how nice it was to have seen her again, moved quietly to the door, said goodbye and departed with a heavy heart.

I had a picnic lunch by the lake in the nearby park, then in the afternoon I walked all the way into Geldrop along the straight featureless arterial road. I went into the church in Geldrop, then called at 48 Eindhovenweg where the Paddings had lived during the war. A boy took me next door (Maria's house) to the neighbours who, he said, had known the Paddings and could tell me more about them. At this house, No. 46, I was given a refreshing glass of beer by the owner who said his wife was out shopping and would be back shortly. It turned out that she, now thirty-eight, was the six-year-old girl who had lived there with her mother during the war. She had a vague childhood recollection that Maria, who had lodged there, left to join the Red Cross as a nurse and was killed. Mrs Padding was also dead and Mr Padding confined in a mental hospital. The Dutch couple at No. 46 waved a friendly goodbye as I left to catch a bus into the centre of Eindhoven. Here I had dinner before calling to see Klaas, as I did not want to intrude upon his evening meal.

I was apprehensive about meeting him as I did not know the circumstances in which he had left his wife. Soon after 8 p.m. I arrived at an elegant house in a quiet, leafy suburb and nervously rang the bell. Flinging open the front door Klaas greeted me with, 'I was hoping it would be you!'

The telephone message delivered to him earlier that day had merely said that 'an Englishman wanted to see him'. During conversation over coffee Klaas explained that, after years of suffering on both sides, his wife's worsening mental condition had become increasingly dangerous for the children and he had taken them away. I did not like to enquire any further. He asked me what brought me to Holland and was amazed that I had taken the trouble to travel all that way in response to 'that crazy postcard'. I said I was worried about Elizabeth's illness and anxious to see them both again after such a long time. We spent a pleasant evening reminiscing over the dark and the light sides of life and then he brought me back to Piuslaan by car.

Klaas was determined that I should make the most of my brief stay in Holland. We went to the eighteenth-century village of Thorn, untouched by the twentieth century except for cars and tourists, to the ancient town of Maastricht and to the village of Budel where the young Paul Kuipers had introduced me to the Resistance leader who was his father. I never saw Elizabeth again and Klaas was reluctant to speak about her when I tried, as tactfully as I could, to give vent to my anxiety.

I also re-visited, on my own, some of the sites I had known during the war: the Manse in Ruusbroeclaan where I had first met the van der Heijden family and the town centre, now unrecognisably a modern shopping precinct in place of the few wartime shops starved of goods.

A kindly Dutchman with whom I entered into conversation while sitting in the park, was intrigued by the reason for my coming back to Holland after the war. It turned out that he and his wife were both teacher training college lecturers, had heard of Goldsmiths' and had travelled extensively in Britain. He was head of the English Department in the Eindhoven college. They invited me to tea and took me to sHertogenbosch, so fiercely fought over, to the daringly modern Provincie Huis, or County Hall, of Noord Brabant, to the new mushroom-shaped Evoluon and to the swimming pool in the ljzeren Man where at Tac HQ in October 1944 His Majesty King George VI held the cushion so lovingly made by a Dutch Elizabeth.

I found Eindhoven in the 1970s – as I was to find Caen and Falaise in the 1980s – so changed, enlarged and refashioned that wartime landmarks, scars and memories were impossible to recapture. It was as though a whole landscape had been melted down and remoulded.

At the end of my stay I had my last meal with Klaas before being driven to the station where he and his young son Jeroen (later to visit me in England) saw me off on the 'Rhein Express'.

Klaas had greeted me as a long-lost friend and we had some pleasant outings together, but I was perturbed by thoughts of the terrible things that can happen to people one has not seen for years, especially to those who have suffered the shocks and privations of war in an occupied country.

In 1981 I received a letter from a stranger, a Mrs Elizabeth Tyzack of Farringdon in Devon, inviting me to the twinning of her small village with one of the smallest villages in Normandy – Secqueville-en-Bessin. She told me that when the English delegation arrived in France to meet their opposite numbers and approve the arrangements for the twinning, two members of the French committee, Monsieur and Madame Hamel, spoke of their friendship with an English soldier whom they had not seen for thirty-seven years and of whom they had lost all trace since they had moved from the village of Blay. In her invitation Mrs Tyzack asked me not to write to the Hamels if I was able to go to Devon, as she wanted to give them a surprise. At the White Horse Inn in Farringdon, where the French had already arrived and were drinking punch, I recognised Marie Louise and François Hamel in a corner. I went up to them. They smiled but did not recognise me. I simply said to Marie Louise,

'C'est moi!'

Tears filled her eyes and ran down her cheeks as we embraced in traditional Normandy fashion (*three* kisses). François grasped my hands with both of his. They had moved from Blay several times and were now in Secqueville-en-Bessin, the place of the twinning. I also had moved from the address which they had known – so we had lost contact.

There followed the parallel reunion in Secqueville, after

which I was taken to Blay for a reception by the mayor and, on the following day, to another welcome in the Hôtel de Ville in Caen. I was given a tour of the Normandy beaches and paid a visit to the D-Day Museum at Arromanches. I was asked to identify the beach on which I had landed in 1944 and stand on it for a photograph, but it was difficult to relate the neat row of modern seaside bungalows to the war-shattered shore which I vaguely remembered having glimpsed in the dusk and clamour of that summer night so long ago. At the British War Cemetery in Bayeux I saw the grave of one of my friends who was with me in the Royal Engineers, my original unit: he had been killed on D-Day. I remembered him grieving over the death of his only brother in the North African desert in 1942. At a service of remembrance in Secqueville-en-Bessin I was given flowers from the community to place at the war memorial to the British servicemen killed there after the Normandy landings.

I met my wartime friends, the Hamels, again at the second twinning event in Farringdon in 1982, and at the thirty-ninth anniversary celebrations of D-Day, when I was invited to recall some memories of Monty and Tac HQ on French radio.

I had kept in touch with Fernand Gennotte ('Nandy') for some years after the war, until his parents moved. Children in my class in the school where I was teaching used to send him stamps and in one of his letters he sent me a philatelic magazine. The Duquesne family with whom I continued to correspond, were unable to discover his whereabouts. In my efforts to trace Fernand's family I wrote to the address of the Belgian philatelic magazine, the only organisation with which I knew he had a connection, and I was at last rewarded. In 1982 I received a letter from his brother, Jean Marie, whom I remembered among the group around Fernand's bed on that evening in September 1944 when I first met the brave young hero. He told me that Nandy had died in 1961 after seventeen and a half painful years on his back. Jean Marie sent me books and articles about his brother and promised to keep in touch with me. He died himself in December 1982.

In 1988 Tournai was unrecognisable with its smart shops, towering office blocks and car-choked roads, but the cobbled streets, retained as part of a government conservation programme, were a reminder of its former identity. It was exciting yet poignant to be revisiting Belgium for the first time after forty-four years, and in September too. I remembered the flowers and the fruits with which we had been bombarded all those years ago.

On this occasion I was the guest of Monsieur and Madame Gergeay (Fernand Gennotte's eldest sister), and had leisure to learn how deeply the Gennotte family had been involved in resistance against the occupying Nazi enemy. Nandy, it appeared, was not the only member of this family to suffer martyrdom. During my nocturnal visit to their home in 1944 in the midst of pressing military duties, there was no time to get better acquainted with other facts of family history, and letters are no substitute for face-to-face confidences. I was to learn that Nandy's great-uncle, General Fernand Gennotte, a veteran of the First World War, (Chevalier de la Légion d'Honneur, Officier de l'Ordre de Léopold, avec palme et croix de guerre, 1914–1918) and a leader of the resistance in touch with London in the Second World War, (Grand Officier de l'Ordre de Léopold avec palme et croix de guerre, 1940) was the only Belgian general to be shot by the enemy. He was arrested on 9 November 1941, deported to Germany, imprisoned, then finally executed at Gordon-Brandeburg on 10 May 1944. He was seventy-one.

After Nandy's escape from forced labour, German patrols came to his home in Moustier in search of him. He had numerous hiding-places in different farms scattered throughout the region. At the approach of the enemy his friends raised the alarm by telephone and he was off to yet another hiding-place. There were some close shaves, as when the fugitive's bicycle was hit by bullets but the pursuing vehicle was halted by an impasse. There were times too when a level crossing gate was deliberately lowered to hinder pursuit. Meanwhile Nandy's mother, after a punitive interrogation and ransacking of her house, was taken to prison in reprisal for her missing son. Her husband, a major in the Belgian army, was a prisoner of war in Germany. Then there was for her the trauma of Nandy's broken body and seventeen years of dedicated nursing. She died in 1985, her husband in 1986.

Returning to the present day, eighty-four-year-old Monsieur Leclercq, former Treasurer of the town of Leuze, the first Belgian to greet Monty's procession at the time of liberation, and to invite me to dinner with his family, was unfortunately ill in hospital in Tournai. I was taken to visit him, but I felt it was presumptuous of an apparent stranger to attempt, under such circumstances, to resurrect those far-distant happenings. It was profoundly moving, however, when he did manage a mute squeeze of my hand and a quasi-military salute before I left his bedside.

Another visit was to Péruwelz, to the Resistance memorial in the town square and to the home of Madame Bachy, widowed in 1987. She was anxious to talk about her husband, Nandy's chef de Résistance, to whose memory she was passionately devoted. She expressed deep disappointment that we had not met before Raymond had died so recently and suddenly after a short illness. She expressed indignation, as did other Belgians of her generation, at the eagerness of some younger compatriots to jump on the Resistance bandwagon at times of national commemoration. These 'enthusiasts' in their early fifties could have been no more than ten years old at the time of the liberation and younger still during the anxious years of secret struggle. I did, however, remember the intrepid Jacques Jansen who at the age of fifteen paid with his life for one act of defiance. It is true that children played their part as carriers of messages and in that capacity ran obvious risks, but parents were naturally wary of exposing their little ones to the daily and nightly dangers of being 'in the Resistance'.

A visit to the Château de la Berlière, now a college for older students, recalled the voices of children singing 'Tipperary' in the elegant assembly hall, which I instantly recognised. Then a call was made to the Duquesne family home, the ancient farmhouse which, after forty-four years, had undergone no apparent change. The cobbled yard with its white-washed walls and old loft ladder seemed to me the same as when I first called at the invitation of the impressive Madame Duquesne, with her six children: Marc, Gérard, Anne-Marie, Robert, Joseph and Jean. The old lady had died, as had Gérard and Joseph. I was greeted by Anne-Marie and Marc, who remembered me, and later by Jean, who was too young in 1944 to form any clear picture of those historic days.

It was to be expected that forty-four years would have taken their toll in the form of sickness, frailty and death. At the monastery in Brussels I learned that Père Edgar had died in 1984, and of the two brave English nuns Mère Ursula, was still living, but Mère Majella had died in 1969 at the age of eighty-one.

Towards the end of my nostalgic stay in Belgium my generous hosts took me on the long journey to Hasselt where I called again at the Ursuline Convent, now renovated and enlarged. The nuns had been prepared by letter and telephone for my proposed visit. There was a current of excitement running through the cloister on our arrival as one sister after another stopped to welcome us. What wonderful preparations they had made. In the quiet parlour we were greeted with an English tea and freshly baked cakes. Mère Ursule, now aged eighty-three, was brought in to have tea with us. She recognised me, called me by name and said she had put on her best habit with a white blouse 'in your honour'. She brought photographs to show me of our British nuns taken prisoner by the Germans. Though I expressed concern that the re-awakening of unpleasant memories might be distressing for her, she cheerfully and in a quiet matter-of-fact voice volunteered a description of the hardships of prison life in the barracks, the starvation diet

221

and the rough bunk beds from which the straw was continually falling out. There were episodes she preferred not to dwell on and I did not press her. Such were their privations and trials that Cardinal Van Roey, the then Primate of Belgium and Archbishop of Malines (Mechelen), negotiated with the occupying power to have all British nuns moved out of the army barracks to Brussels, though they were still prisoners of the Germans and suffering the restraints of wartime internment.

I often wondered what had happened to Major O'Brien with whom I had shared what must surely have been the most momentous and historic experience of both our lives: the delivery of the final terms of surrender to Field Marshal Keitel at the Oberkommando der Wehrmacht in Flensburg on 7 May 1945. It was through the BBC that we met again after forty years when VE-Day was commemorated on television on 8 May 1985. It was thrilling to meet again and to confirm that our memories of the great event were intact. We differed over only one small detail concerning our awesome entry into Keitel's private office. Sir Richard O'Brien, as he is now, said that we turned right. My memory tells me that we turned left, but I don't think this little difference will alter the course of history.

Another more solemn last connection with Tactical Headquarters itself was on 1 April 1976 at St George's Chapel, Windsor Castle, when I attended the funeral service of Field Marshal the Viscount Montgomery of Alamein.

Sitting in St George's Chapel, I watched on giant television screens, the slow procession of the coffin from the barracks through the crowded, hushed streets of Windsor. The band of the Grenadier Guards played the 'Dead March in Saul'. At the very moment when the cortège reached the west end of the chapel, the doors were opened wide and we inside saw the televised coffin on the screen become the real coffin moving slowly past us down the aisle, bearing on it the sword and baton of Field Marshal Montgomery and his famous beret. At the precise moment when the band outside finished playing, the organ inside the chapel picked up the sound and the funeral service began.

Outside the chapel banks of many-coloured flowers from all over the world covered the smooth lawns in the spring sunshine. I thought of the many miles of war-ravaged land travelled by this man who with single-minded obstinacy cut through all objections to forward his own clearly perceived plan with sincerity, simplicity and unfaltering, infuriating, reassuring self-confidence.

I thought too of the world he had left, a world which he had helped to save from the Nazis but which remains a world where falsehood, hypocrisy and double standards go hand in hand with power, and alas, where new weapons make our impressive D-Day *matériel* look like children's toys. Such a world does not seem to be worth the sacrifice of one human life, yet those who suffered did believe that their cause was just, and a great evil was destroyed by brave men and women. There is still some good left and those of us who are growing old in places made safe from tyranny give thanks to them.

INDEX